BUILDING
THE UQBAR DINGHY
with the Stitch-and-Glue Technique

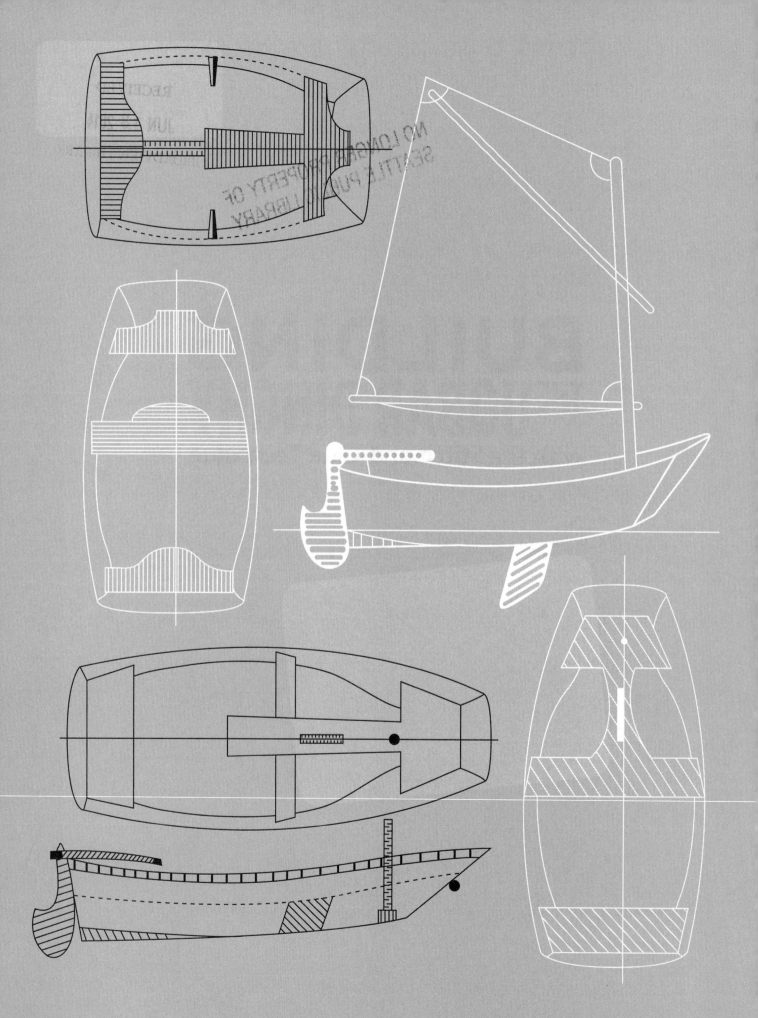

BUILDING
THE UQBAR DINGHY
with the Stitch-and-Glue Technique

REDJEB JORDANIA

INTERNATIONAL MARINE / McGRAW-HILL EDUCATION
Camden, Maine • New York • Chicago • San Francisco • Lisbon • London • Madrid •
Mexico City • Milan • New Delhi • San Juan • Seoul • Singapore • Sydney • Toronto

1 2 3 4 5 6 7 8 9 10 11 12 QVS/QVS 1 9 8 7 6 5 4
ISBN 978-0-07-183101-7
MHID 0-07-183101-0
E ISBN 0-07-182965-2

Library of Congress Cataloging-in-Publication Data is available from the Library of Congress.

McGraw-Hill Education books are available at special quantity discounts to use as premiums and sales promotions or for use in corporate training programs. To contact a representative, please e-mail us at bulksales@mcgraw-hill.com.

This book is printed on acid-free paper.

All photos are from the author's collection except where noted.

Questions regarding the content of this book should be addressed to www.internationalmarine.com

Questions regarding the ordering of this book should be addressed to
McGraw-Hill Education
Customer Service Department
P.O. Box 547
Blacklick, OH 43004
Retail customers: 1-800-262-4729
Bookstores: 1-800-722-4726

Contents

The Uqbar

The *pram*-nosed rowing or sailing *dinghy* has long been a favorite of sailors for its stability, large carrying capacity, and seaworthy characteristics. Our Uqbar family of prams further enhances those qualities through superior design and the use of modern materials and construction techniques. (Note: Italicized terms are defined in the Brief Glossary or the Extended Glossary, or both.)

Uqbars are built of ash, pine, and marine mahogany or fir plywood held together with *epoxy* products—a composite construction that yields what is in effect a one-piece hull that cannot leak and requires almost no maintenance.

6', 7', 8', and 10' superlight prams even you can build!

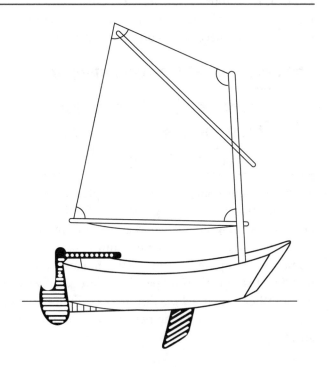

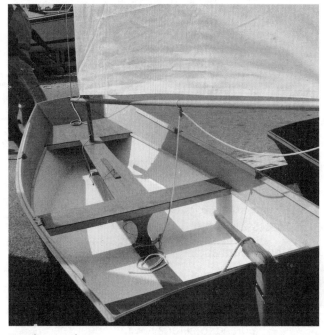

Ready to sail.

The Uqbar Name

The name *Uqbar* is borrowed from *Tlön, Uqbar, Orbis Tertius*, a short story by the twentieth-century Argentine writer Jorge Luis Borges. In the story, an encyclopedia article about a mysterious country called *Uqbar* is the first indication of a massive conspiracy of intellectuals to imagine and thereby create a world known as *Tlön*.

In much the same way, I imagined, designed, and built a *trimaran* and its tender, which I baptized *Tlön* and *Uqbar*, thus creating my own new world in which to escape the humdrum of our everyday universe.

Estimated Materials and Costs

Costs will vary widely, of course, depending on which model you build, the type of soft- and hardwoods you purchase, and a number of other variables. However, below is a rough estimate of the cost of materials used to build a rowing model Uqbar.

Epoxy: about $40 per quart, or $160 for a kit that includes 1 gallon, plus pumps, thickeners, and fiberglass tape.

Plywood:

LUAN (Philippine mahogany)—about $20 per 4′ × 8′ Luan sheet. Luan usually has a solid core material sandwiched between two layers of veneer. In total, you'll spend about $50 when using Luan.

EXTERIOR GRADE GOOD TWO SIDES—a good alternative to Luan, and necessary for U10 since Luan does not usually come in 4′ × 10′ sheets. About $31 per 4′ × 8′ sheet, and $40 per 4′ × 10′ sheet.

MARINE—quite a bit more expensive, and not necessary. About $45 per 4′ × 8′ sheet.

Other Wood: about $40.

Fasteners: very few fasteners are used, but set aside about $25.

The grand total for a rowing model, then, is about $300 to $375, to which must be added the cost of oars and oarlocks. These range from $12/pair (zinc) to $52/pair (bronze).

If you're building a sailing model, you'll also need to include in your estimate the cost of spars, sail, pintles and gudgeons, and lines.

SPARS and LINES: about $45.

PINTLES/GUDGEONS (two of each): prices range from $15 to $54 each.

SAIL: about $250 for U8 and U7, or $300 for U10.

Keep in mind that even if you're building a sailing or motoring dinghy you'll want to have oars (or at least paddles) aboard in case of emergency.

Uqbars feature a *rockered* bottom, a sweeping *sheer* line with high *freeboard*, and flaring *topsides* with a rounded *forefoot* achieved by bending the hull panels in two and even three dimensions, thereby imparting even more strength to the materials. The wooden Uqbars will not sink, even absent special flotation mechanisms, such as foam blocks or airtight compartments.

Since the prototype was launched in 1976, Uqbars have been sailed, towed, rowed, and motored in a great variety of places and circumstances. They are readily car-topped and single-handedly carried ashore or hoisted on deck. They are extensively used as primary boats or as yacht tenders roomy enough for useful loads, yet compact enough to fit aboard most small yachts, while doubling as fun sailing *dinks* for young and old alike.

Uqbar and the Home Builder

If you can handle a pencil, a drill, a jigsaw, and a few hand tools, you can build an Uqbar quickly and well, as evidenced by the many amateur-built Uqbars plying the seven seas from Homer, Alaska, to the Sea of Japan. This consistent success of even beginners is made possible by Uqbar's design and materials, and by the stitch-and-glue method of construction, which bypasses many work-intensive boatbuilding methods.

In building Uqbar, no painstaking joinery work is needed. For instance, instead of a wooden *chine* with its changing bevels, we use a "liquid" chine consisting of epoxy putty *filleted* into the seams.

This is possible because, unlike other glues, epoxy fills gaps for a 100%-strong bond and needs no clamping pressure for gluing: contact is enough. The result is, in effect, a one-piece boat—one that will never leak.

The Stitch-and-Glue Technique, or . . .

"You can build 'em faster than you can varnish 'em!" (Well, not quite!)

Stitch-and-glue construction is a simple technique for building strong boats using *Luan* (Philippine mahogany) or marine-grade plywood and a minimum number of tools. It also requires minimum skills. No ribs or framework is required, as is normally the case with boatbuilding. Instead, plywood panels are butted up against one another and attached—in this case with metal or plastic wire-ties—and then permanently bonded with an epoxy *fillet*.

Plywood for Uqbar

Our philosophy for building Uqbar is to go for the inexpensive yet good. We recommend top-grade Luan (Philippine mahogany) plywood since it combines good quality with low price. However, it is not always easy to purchase locally (see Sources of Materials, page 80), so the alternative is either fir marine plywood (relatively expensive) or, more economical and just as practical, fir exterior grade good two sides.

As you would expect, there are limitations to this sort of construction. The number of vessel shapes and styles one can create using sheets of plywood is finite: in general, one cannot use stitch-and-glue techniques to form complex shapes, round bottoms, and so on. However, when building a relatively simple boat such as a dinghy or canoe, those limitations are more than offset by the ease, simplicity, and affordability of construction—not to mention the strength and structural integrity of the resulting vessel.

Although there are variations, in general, the stitch-and-glue process consists of the following steps. As noted above, the plywood panels are cut to exact size. Using metal or plastic wire-ties, the parts are then literally "stitched" together to form the boat itself. (Early stitching systems used fishing line to connect the parts. Thousands of years before that, native Laplanders and others used leather cord as stitching material for similar "sewn boats" made of skin, and then they waterproofed the seams with clay.) The parts are then permanently joined and the edges sealed on the inside with epoxy putty. The outside seams are then covered with *fiberglass* tape. After the epoxy cures, final touches (seats, *rubrails*, etc.) are added. The result is a simple, inexpensive, strong boat that can be built by anyone who can use a jigsaw and a ruler or measuring tape.

To recap, the five basic steps are quite simple:

– CUT all parts to exact shape with the help of our cutting diagrams.
– STITCH the hull panels together with metal or plastic wire-ties.
– GLUE the panels together by spreading epoxy putty over the wires on the inside.
– SNIP OFF the wire ends on the outside and fair.
– EPOXY fiberglass tape on the outside of the seams.

U8 and U10 sprit-rigged Uqbars on the beach.

OLD SAILORS
NEVER DIE ...
THEY JUST GET A
LITTLE DINGHY .....

COME TO THE CHRISTENING
AT
SATURDAY,
21 MAY
FROM 1600
REGRETS ONLY

Et voilà! Time of assembly varies with the skill of the builder. As a rough guide, an Uqbar 8 hull can be assembled in approximately 6 to 8 hours, and the whole boat in one long weekend.

Your Path to Success:
How to Use This Book

This book contains plenty of background material about the stitch-and-glue boatbuilding technique, as well as a step-by-step guide to building an Uqbar dinghy. In addition, it provides information (including plans and cutting diagrams) specific to each of the four models of dinghy discussed herein. Finally—but perhaps most importantly—the book includes a captioned Visual Guide (page 9) that will take you graphically through the process; as much as anything, the guide will help familiarize you with the technique.

We recommend that you skim through the entire book before getting to work, and even before deciding which model you'd like to build. As you read, you may come across some unfamiliar terms: most of these are defined in either the Brief Glossary (page 6) or the Extended Glossary (page 77). (The terms are set in italics the first time they are used in this book.) Take the time to look up terms with which you're unfamiliar *before* you start building.

After familiarizing yourself with the book and some of the terminology, walk through the Visual Guide (page 9). Doing so will give you a good idea of the sort of work involved—and also just how easy it really is to build an Uqbar.

You might also want to read the two short Uqbar-building articles (pages 83–85). The first describes building Uqbar in a supervised workshop; the second describes the process of building Uqbar at home.

If you're looking for information about sources of materials used, see page 80.

Everything make sense? It should; it's really not that complicated. If you can follow directions, measure, and draw a straight line, you can build a great boat, at minimal cost, in a weekend.

Building Your Dinghy

Ready to get started?

Now it's time to decide which model of Uqbar suits your circumstances. Read carefully the description for each of the four sizes offered to help you make a decision. There is little difference in cost or working time among the models, so don't let those factors sway you. The main decision is choosing between rowing and sailing models; building a sailboat involves additional work, and also additional expense for the sail itself and the associated gear. (Note that except for U6, any rowing/motoring model can be modified into a sailing dinghy.)

Next, assemble the materials per the list provided for each model, and make sure you have the appropriate tools. The only absolutely necessary power tools are a simple jigsaw with a plywood-cutting blade, and an or-

A completed Uqbar dinghy being used as a tender.

> ## *"The amazing thing is that in a very short time—2 hours—the boat was assembled, ready to be glued!"*
>
> (See article, page 83.)

dinary drill. If you happen to have a sander or a circular saw for cutting straight lines, all the better.

When you are ready to start work, follow the step-by-step instructions on pages 58–76. The same set of instructions is used for all models, interpolating instructions for the different sizes as explained in the appropriate chapter. The instructions are very detailed since they are written with the inexperienced builder in mind. In fact they are so detailed that they can be a bit confusing. The trick is to start working without looking too much ahead, or at least not worrying too much about anything confusing that you might see if you *do* look ahead. As you get going, things will become clear. Nothing replaces the hands-on process! For visual help, refer to the relevant photos in the Visual Guide, page 9. (Of course, the experienced boatbuilder can skip over many of the details.)

You may prefer to concentrate the work in one or two weekends, or spread it out for as long as you wish, as shown in the articles on pages 83–85. The only time you must act quickly is when you use epoxy for coating, filleting, or gluing, because epoxy has a limited *pot life*. Depending on the air temperature, a batch of mixed epoxy can become unusable in as little as 15 minutes.

Brief Glossary

Every trade has its own specialized vocabulary. Here are explanations of some of the terms most commonly used in boatbuilding. Note that a more extensive glossary is found in Appendix A (page 77). Unusual terms are italicized in their first use in the text—that is your clue to look them up in one of the glossaries.

Aft. The back part of the boat, or toward the back of the boat.

Athwartships. Across.

Batten. A long, thin, flexible piece of wood used to re-

inforce something, such as a wooden structure. Often refers to a piece inserted in the leech of a sail, but here mostly used in the former sense.

Bevel. A cut at any angle other than 90 degrees that extends the entire thickness of the plank.

Bottom Runners. Long softwood battens running fore and aft on the underside of the boat to protect it when pulling it up a beach and to improve tracking while underway.

Chamfer. A cut at an angle other than 90 degrees that does not extend the entire thickness of the plank.

Chine. The angled piece shaped and placed between the outside edge of the bottom plank and the bottom edge of the side plank. In our case we replace that piece with an epoxy fillet.

Daggerboard. A centerboard in small sailboats that is emplaced or removed vertically through a well or trunk.

Doubler. A piece of wood attached to planking to "double" its thickness as a way of adding strength.

Fair. To smooth.

Fore. Short for *forward*; the front, or toward the front, of a boat.

Forefoot. The area of a pram-nosed dinghy where the bottom panel and the bow transom are joined.

Inwale. The long, thin batten that reinforces the sheer on the inside.

Jig. A device or frame used to hold work and to guide tools being used on the work.

Keelson. A plank (here, plywood) that extends the whole length of the boat on the inside to reinforce the keel.

King Plank. Here, the plank extending between the center and forward seats, to which the top of the daggerboard trunk is secured on sailing versions of Uqbar.

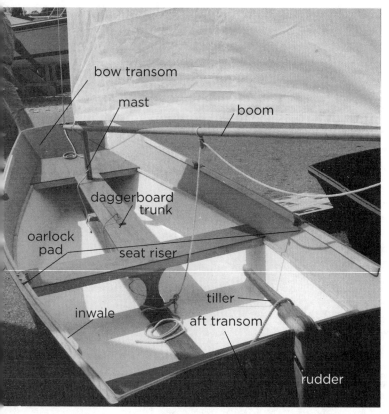

Interior of an Uqbar dinghy with key parts labeled.

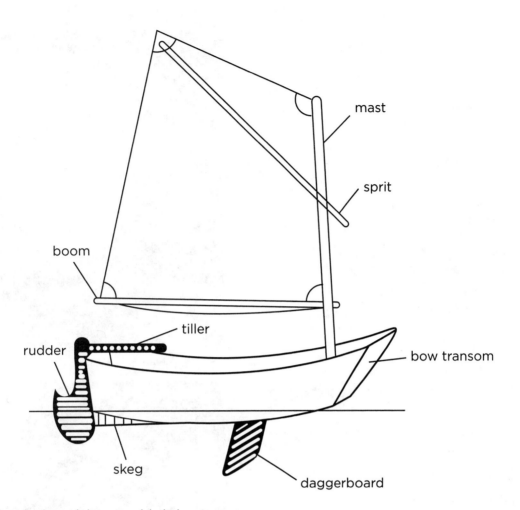

mast

sprit

boom

tiller

rudder

bow transom

skeg

daggerboard

A sail-rigged Uqbar dinghy with key parts labeled.

Knee. A piece of timber naturally or artificially bent for use in supporting structures coming together at an angle. Traditionally knees were fashioned out of naturally bent tree roots or branches.

Lofting. The art of drawing a boat and parts full size. In our case we draw the parts directly on the plywood stock.

Port. The left side of a vessel when looking toward the front, or bow.

Pot Life. The length of time an epoxy mix will remain viable and useful; once it begins to harden, a new batch must be mixed.

Rubrail. The long, thin batten that reinforces and protects the sheer on the outside.

Seat Riser. A batten fastened to the side planks and on the *transoms*, to which the seats will be attached.

Sheer. The top edge of the side plank.

Skeg. A small fin fitted aft of the keel to protect the rudder and propeller and improve steering and tracking.

Starboard. The right side of a vessel when looking toward the front, or bow.

Strongback. Temporary scaffolding used to hold parts together while working.

Building a Scale Model of UQBAR 8

This 8" Uqbar model was built by Will Backman, of Maine, preparatory to building a full-size pram-dinghy.

He used the cutting diagrams for U8, scaling down the dimensions (1 foot = 1 inch), and the step-by-step instructions. It's a fun project to acquaint you with the boat, or to share with a youngster in your life.

Materials

All materials were purchased at a local craft store.

___One sheet of 2' x 3' $\frac{1}{32}$"-thin birch mini-ply-wood—it is thin enough to cut with scissors.

___A roll of thin copper wire.

___Round $\frac{5}{32}$" dowel to serve as a mast and one slightly thinner round dowel to cut into the boom and sprit.

___Elmers Wood Glue.

___Square $\frac{1}{16}$" balsa battens for the seat risers and rub rails.

___Wood clothespins for clamps.

___Cloth for sail.

___String for rigging.

___Brushes, paint, and varnish.

The assembled hull showing the thin wire and glue.

Ready to sail. (Well, almost!)

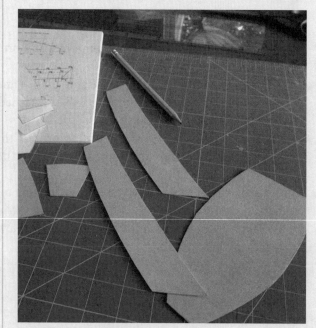

Parts for the hull are cut. Use the plans in the book and scale them down–1 foot = 1 inch.

"It is amazing how a few flat pieces of wood can suddenly become the curved shape of a boat."
—Will Backman

Visual Guide

Building Uqbar with the Stitch-and-Glue Technique

This visual guide to the stitch-and-glue technique of boatbuilding is based on the construction of our Uqbar prams. Please study it carefully to help familiarize yourself with the process. (For the actual construction of your dinghy, use the step-by-step building instructions that begin on page 58.)

Materials are 5.5 mm (or ¼") Luan or marine-grade plywood, with ash and pine for trim and reinforcing members. Fasteners are #4 copper wire or any other soft wire-ties or plastic ties, fiberglass tape, and WEST SYSTEM epoxy products. The few metal fasteners used include two lag bolts to anchor the *skeg* and a few screws to hold the seats in position while the glue sets. Temporary screws can be used in lieu of clamps, if necessary, in particular to glue on the *seat risers*. If desired, the screws can be left in place, in which case they should be the non-rusting type; stainless steel, brass, or bronze screws work well.

The stitch-and-glue technique is extremely simple and forgiving. As noted, no painstaking joinery is necessary, and small gaps can be filled for a 100% bond with epoxy putty. For the Uqbar prams, no temporary *jig* or *strongback* is needed. The boat is self-aligning, provided you have prepared accurately cut plywood panels by following exactly the detailed plans provided in the step-by-step instructions and in the chapter detailing the construction of the model you've opted to build.

Once cut, the matching panels' edges are slightly *chamfered* to help alignment. It is then a good idea to coat the panels with epoxy before assembly, particularly the inside faces.

Coating the outside is best accomplished after the boat has been built. The boat can be used immediately, with just its epoxy coating, but you would have to protect that coating from the sun's ultraviolet waves after the first season. A good marine varnish will do the trick, although some customers prefer to keep the inside *bright* but paint the outside. Others paint the whole hull but keep *transoms* and seats bright. Your choice!

Assembling the Hull

1

Threading the wire-ties through matching holes, side to bottom plank seam, aft. The transom is already wired to the bottom. Note the can containing precut wire-ties.

2

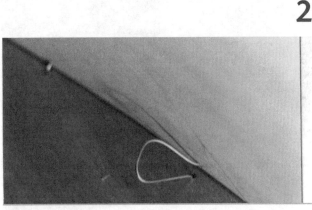

The side planks are now near-vertical, attached to the transom. The wire-ties are pushed through from the inside.

3

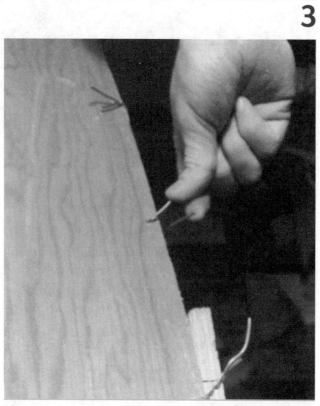

Twisting together the wire ends on the outside. This can generally be accomplished by hand. Note again that the twisted portion of the wire-ties is on the *outside* of the boat. (The twisted portion will be snipped off.)

4

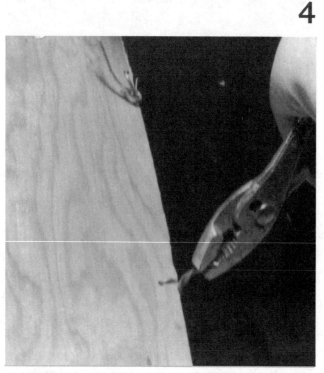

Tightening. Exerting the pressure needed to bring the parts together requires the use of pliers or a similar tool.

5

An inside view of the three-panel assembly.

6

Looking aft at the partially assembled hull.

7

Looking forward prior to installing the *bow transom*.

8

An inside view of the bow transom assembly.

9

An outside view of the bow transom assembly. Note the additional wire-ties used to help counteract the *bending moment*.

Gluing on the Seat Risers

10

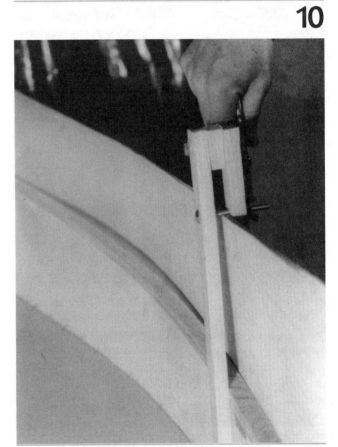

A single homemade clamp holds the riser against the side plank in its approximate position.

11 and 12

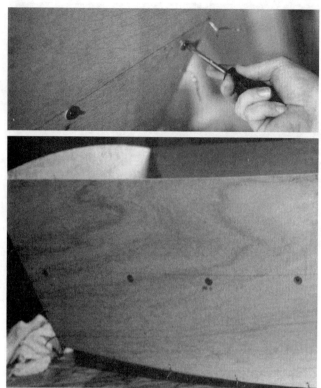

Instead of clamps, you can use temporary screws driven through washers to hold risers firmly against the side plank while the glue sets. (Use #6 screws, round head, 5/8".) For correct positioning of the screws, note the line corresponding to the top of the riser inside.

Filleting

13

Final wire-tie tightening by using a mallet and large screwdriver to push the wire as close to the wood panels as feasible.

14

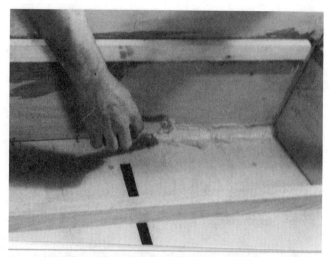

Spreading the epoxy putty into the seam. Note in the foreground the spreader holding the side planks at the proper distance. At this point, it's important that the boat be aligned correctly; once the epoxy fillets set, the dinghy's form is permanent.

15

Removing the excess epoxy with a shaped squeegee results in a neat, even fillet. The best fillet is the smallest one possible, so don't overapply the epoxy.

16

The *forefoot* is reinforced with a length of fiberglass tape pushed into the wet fillet and saturated with clear epoxy. Note that the fillet must still be wet when the tape is applied, so work quickly but carefully.

Fiberglassing the Outside Seams

17

After the fillets have cured, the wire is snipped off.

18

Knocking off the outside edges with a block plane.

19

Finish rounding the edges with coarse sandpaper (#40). Note the well-shaped corner.

20

Overlapping lengths of 2"-wide fiberglass tape that were precut and set aside.

21

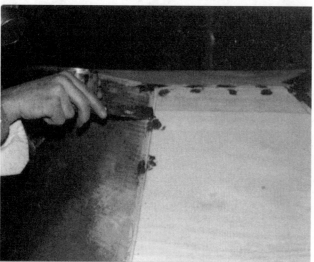

Holes, gouges, and cracks are filled with not-too-thick epoxy putty.

22

The outside seam is immediately painted with clear epoxy, distributing the excess putty evenly.

23

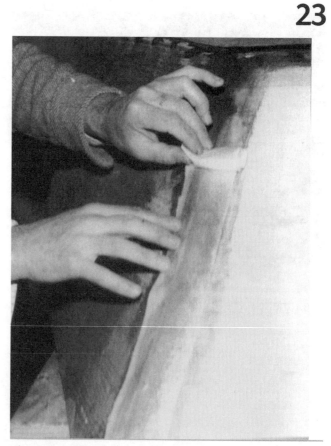

The tape is unrolled into the resin.

24

Stretch the tape to avoid wrinkles or bubbles.

25

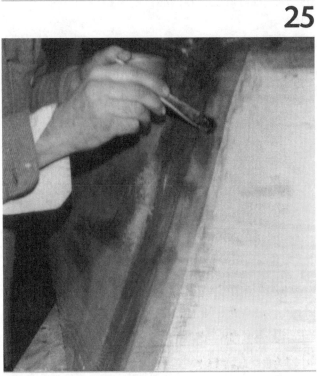

Saturate the tape with clear epoxy. A pinch of *colloidal silica* (generally available wherever you purchased your epoxy) in the resin will help fill in the weave.

Installing the Transom Doublers

26

This is best done while the tape is still wet, in order to avoid sanding. Just hold the bow and aft *doublers* in position with clamps (or screws) while the glue sets.

27

After cure, the doublers' edges are trimmed even with the side plank.

28

An outside view of the aft transom/side junction, showing how the *rubrail* overlaps the transom doubler.

Gluing on the Skeg and Bottom Runners

29 and 30

The skeg is epoxied into its groove (lower photo), and the runners directly onto the bottom. Note that while the glue cures, everything is held in place with a combination of clamps, *battens* and weights, and screws.

Installing the Seats and Seat Supports

31

The center seat is cut exactly to size and is installed first. The forward and aft seats are then trimmed to fit. All seats are held in position with #8 × ¾" non-rusting screws.

32

The forward seat: Note the small C-clamps holding the supports in position while the glue sets.

33

A close-up, inside: Note how the corner of the seat has been rounded to fit around the epoxy fillet.

34

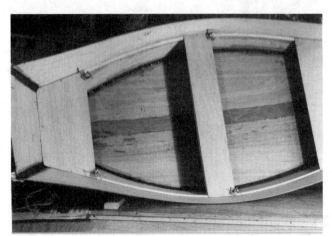

General view, inside the Uqbar 8 rowing model.

At this point, the rowing model is finished except for the *inwale* and *oarlock* pads and any finishing touches, such as painting and varnishing to taste. If you intend to use an outboard motor, then the transom assembly needs to be reinforced to better resist the thrust of the motor. (See "Knees" in the step-by-step instructions.)

In addition, the sailing model requires the *king plank*, *daggerboard* trunk, and *mast step*, plus the daggerboard, rudder and tiller, mast, boom, appropriate hardware, lines, and sail.

Uqbar 8
The Maximum Dinghy
Row/Sail/Motor

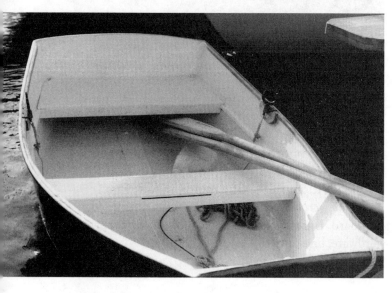

The first of the Uqbar family, U8 was originally conceived as a tender for the designer's own trimaran, *Tlön*. Since multihulls do not take kindly to weight, the first Uqbar had to be as light as possible and at the same time combine large capacity, compactness, and good handling characteristics, including towing at relatively high speed. From the very beginning, Uqbar met all expectations, and other sailors started wanting their own. The Back 'n Forth Company was founded to satisfy the demand.

Uqbar 8 is 7'10" long, 48" wide, 17" deep, and weighs only 55 lbs. She carries three adults and gear easily—four in a pinch if the waters are calm. She features a sweeping sheer line, flaring topsides, and a strongly rockered bottom, a necessity in pram-nosed dinghies, since both transoms should be kept out of the water when underway in order to minimize drag.

The sailing model offers a simple sprit rig, a kick-up rudder, and a daggerboard for lateral resistance. A single clip-on leeboard with kick-up blade is offered as an optional alternative to the daggerboard (for more on the leeboard, see page 32).

Uqbar 8 is large enough to be enjoyed as a primary boat that can be readily car-topped, even on a convertible, yet small enough to be used as an efficient yacht tender.

Chapter Contents

Description/Specifications

L.O.A. (LENGTH) 7' 10"
BEAM (WIDTH) 48"
DRAFT 17" WITH DAGGERBOARD DOWN
WEIGHT 55 LBS.
CAPACITY 3+ ADULTS

Building Uqbar 8

Please go to page 58, "Building Uqbar." These step-by-step instructions are written specifically for U8, so you can follow them exactly.

Building Materials and Other Supplies

Wood

Plywood

___ ¼" top-grade Luan, marine, or exterior good two sides
___ Sailing model: 3 sheets 4' × 8'
___ Rowing model: 2½ sheets
Laminate double thickness where ½" is indicated.

Pine

___ ¾" × 1½": 20' (seat risers)
___ ½" × ¾" × 8': 4 pieces
___ 1 plank ¾" × 4" × 24" (forward seat riser/pad for eyebolt)

Ash

___ 4 strips ⅝" × 1" × 8' (for rubrails and inwales)
___ 1 plank ¾" × 3" × 32" (for the skeg)

Sailboats Only

___ Ash: 1" × 1¼" × 48" (for tiller and tiller cheeks)
___ Clothes-hanger stock (i.e., dowel rods of fir or pine such as one might use in a closet) for spars:
____ 1⅝" diameter × 8' (for the mast)
____ 1⅜" diameter × 6'6" (for the boom)
____ 1⅛" diameter × 6'6" (for the *sprit*)

Fasteners

___ Bare copper wire, #4, 7-strand, 6' (yields over 100 wire-ties); obtain from your favorite electrical supply or local hardware store
___ **OR** round plastic wire-tires (100 needed)
___ 2 galvanized lag bolts, ¼" × 1½", with oversize washers
___ Various temporary wood screws, #8 × 1" and 1¼"

Epoxy Products

___ WEST SYSTEM epoxy products (available in many building supplies stores) or other brand. (Note: always use mask and protective gloves)
___ 3 quarts epoxy resin plus hardener (rowing models: 2 quarts)
___ Fiberglass tape: 2" or 3" wide × 30'
___ 8 oz. microfibers
___ 5 oz. filleting blend or microballoons
___ 1 oz. colloidal silica (optional)
___ 6 dozen disposable acid brushes or similar (so-called because they're the type of small, inexpensive brush often used to brush on acid, or flux, when soldering; useful for spreading epoxy of various thicknesses)
___ 6 pairs disposable sponge roller sleeves
___ 6 small plastic squeegees

Hardware and Miscellaneous

All Models

___ 2 pairs oarlocks
___ 1 galvanized eyebolt, ⅜" × 2" (a so-called tow-eye)

Sailboats Only

___ 1 bronze screw, #12 × 3" (for head of sprit)
___ 2 bronze carriage bolts, ⅜" × 3" and ⅜" × 2" (rudder blade and tiller pivots)
___ 1 bronze carriage bolt, ⅜" × 3" (for optional leeboard pivot)
___ 2 pairs pintles and gudgeons with appropriate bolts and finishing washers (stainless steel or bronze)
___ 2 small blocks and 3 small cleats (for ¼" line)
___ 20' of ⅛" lacing line and 36' of ¼" Dacron line
___ SAIL: 35 sq. ft., 3 oz. or 3.5 oz. Dacron (obtain from your local sailmaker, or request quotes through the Internet)

Cutting Diagrams
Bottom Plank

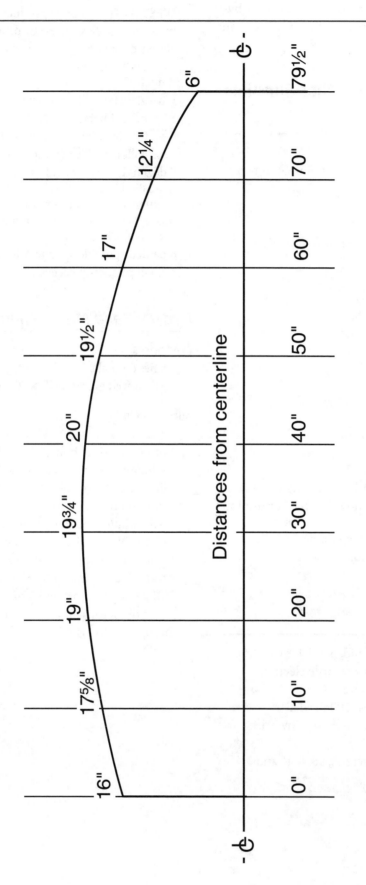

A half-breadth view of the bottom plank of the U8 dinghy.

Side Plank (2 needed)

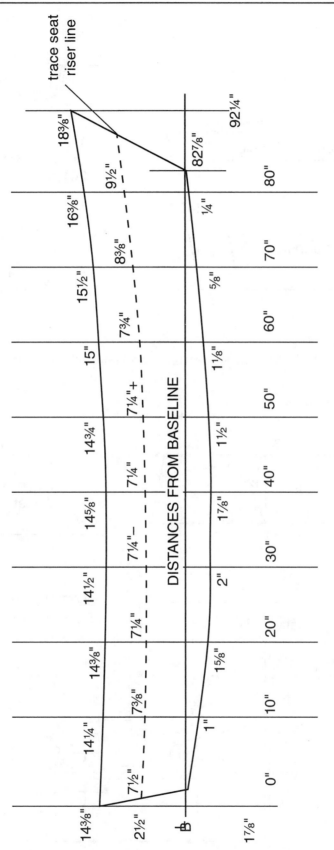

Obviously, you'll need two of these side planks, one for each side as specified.

Bow and Aft Transoms

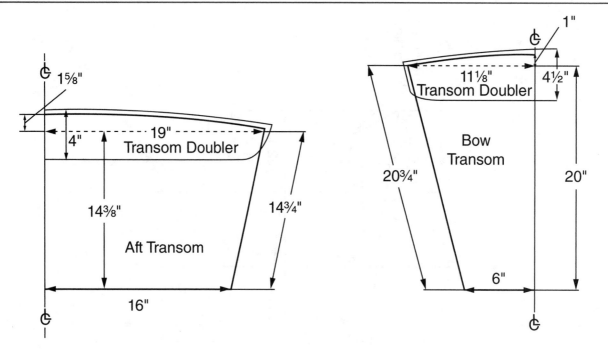

The bow and aft transoms. Note the transom doublers used to add strength to the structure.

Seats and King Plank

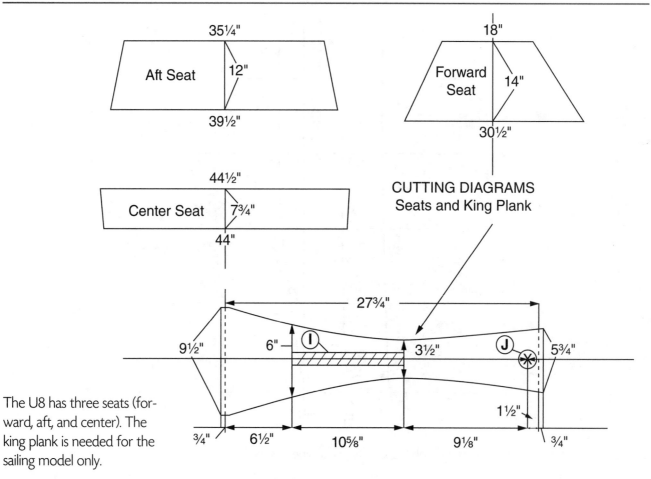

The U8 has three seats (forward, aft, and center). The king plank is needed for the sailing model only.

Daggerboard Trunk

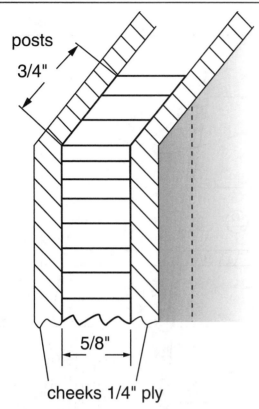

posts
3/4"

5/8"

cheeks 1/4" ply

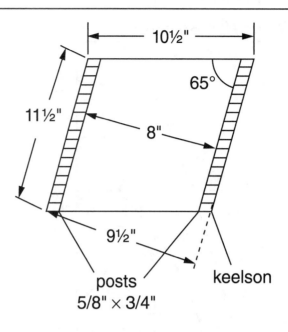

10½"

65°

11½"

8"

9½"

posts
5/8" × 3/4"

keelson

The cheeks, made of ¼" plywood and two ⅝" × ¾" pine posts, form the casing (or trunk) to hold the daggerboard and from which it will be lowered into the water when needed.

Daggerboard

Blade: ½" plywood
Stop: The stop will show as it rests atop the trunk, so use a nice-looking ½" × 2½" × 12¼" piece of wood. Any type will do, but coat the stop with epoxy to avoid rot and discoloration.

The stop is fastened on top of the blade with epoxy and #6 × 1½" screws pushed into oversize pilot holes filled with epoxy.

The handle consists of a 15" length of ¼" Dacron or similar rope pushed into 1½"-deep holes filled with epoxy.

The daggerboard is raised and lowered with the aid of a rope handle. A 12¼"-wide piece of wood is used as a stop to arrest the daggerboard's descent.

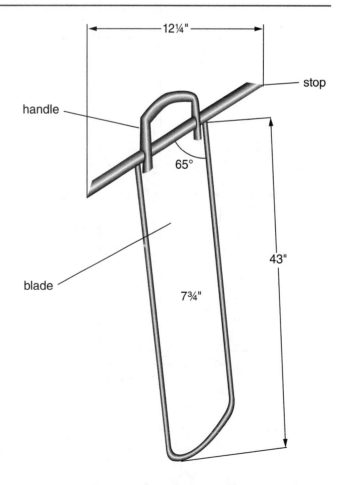

12¼"

stop

handle

65°

blade

7¾"

43"

Plans and Key to Plans

Profile and Half-Breadth

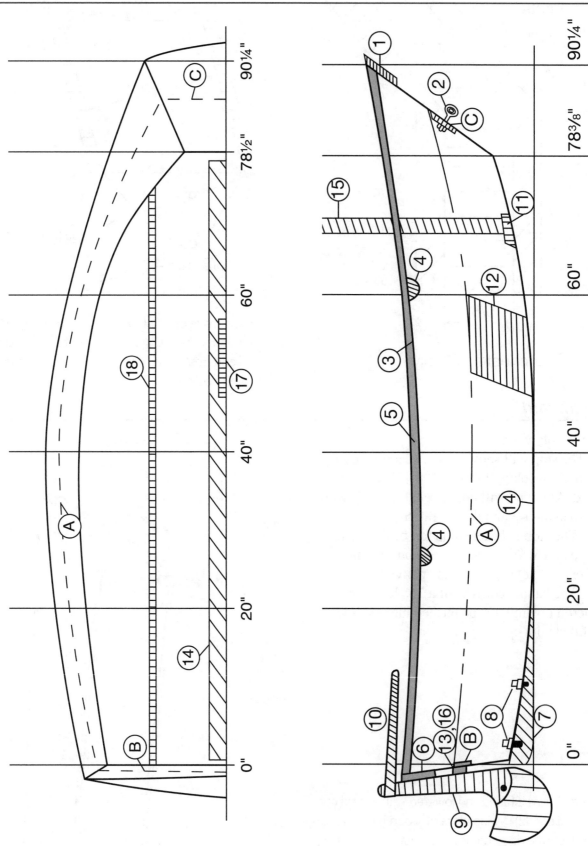

Key to Illustration (page 24)

1. Bow transom doubler, ½" plywood.
2. Tow-eye, ⁵⁄₁₆" × 2" galvanized shoulder eyebolt with washer (C).
3. Rubrail, ⅝" × ¾" ash or equivalent.
4. Oarlock pads, ½" plywood.
5. Inwale, ½" × ¾" ash or equivalent.
6. Aft transom doubler, ½" plywood.
7. Skeg, ¾" × 3" × 32" ash or oak.
8. Lag bolts, ¼" × 1½" galvanized + oversize washers.
9. Kick-up rudder, ⅜" plywood. OR blade and packing piece, ⅛" aluminum, flanges same or ⅜" plywood.
10. Tiller and tiller cheeks, ¾" ash stock.
11. Mast step 2½" × 3½" × 5" pine, with 1⅝"-diameter hole.
12. Daggerboard trunk, ¼" plywood and ⅝" × ¾" pine posts.
13. Lower gudgeon pad, ½" plywood.
14. Keelson, ¼" × 3¾" plywood.
15. Mast, 1⅝" diameter.
16. Sailboats only: pad for lower gudgeon, ½" × 2" × 4".
17. Daggerboard slot.
18. Bottom runner.

Seats and King Plank at Seat-Riser Level

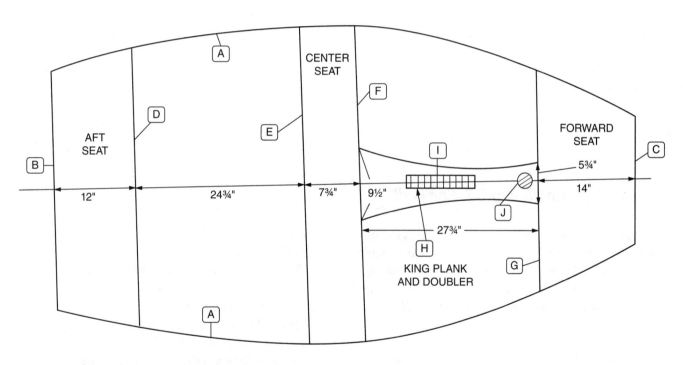

U8 has three seats—forward, aft, and center—resting on 1½" × ¾" supports.

A. Side seat risers, ½" × ¾" parting strips, beveled 15 degrees on top.
B. Aft seat riser, 1½" × ¾" #2 pine, beveled 10 degrees on top.
C. Forward seat riser and tow-eye pad, 4" × ¾", beveled 55 degrees.

D, E, F, and G. Seat supports, 1½" × ¾", double-beveled and notched at each end to fit around seat risers.
H. King plank and doubler.
I. Slot for daggerboard trunk.
J. 1⅝"-diameter hole for mast.

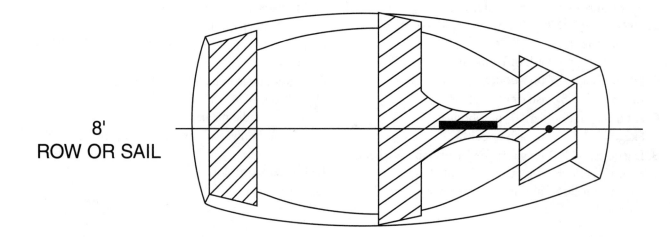

8'
ROW OR SAIL

A bird's-eye view of the U8, configured for rowing or sailing.

Sailing Rigs for U8 and U7: Spritsail

The spritsail is a form of four-sided sail. This rig supports the *leech* of the sail by means of a spar or spars named a sprit. The forward end of the sprit is attached to the mast but bisects the face of the sail, with the after end of the sprit attaching to the peak of the sail.

Key to Illustration

A. Mast, 1⅝" diameter × 8'.

B. Boom, 1⅜" diameter × 6'6".

C. Sprit, 1⅛" diameter × 6'6".

D. *Snotter assembly:* The control line is dead-ended at 1, goes through a hole in the mast at 2, thence to cleat I on mast.

E. Tip of sprit: A large bronze screw (#12 × 2½") with the top cut off and rounded (1) is pushed into an oversize pilot hole filled with epoxy (2).

F and G. The sail is permanently *bent* to the mast

with a lacing line dead-ended through hole at F, and laced down.

H. The downhaul goes around the mast once and down to cleat I.

I. Cleats for downhaul and for snotter.

J. *Clew* and *tack* are laced to boom. The sail is otherwise loose-footed.

K. *Blocks:* As light as possible, since your head will be close by!

L. The sheet is dead-ended at M to a ring around the rope traveler (or a simple bowline), thence *reeved* through blocks K, and back into the sailor's hand.

M. Ring, brass (or bowline).

N. Rope traveler.

O. The rope traveler is dead-ended through holes at O with figure-8 knots.

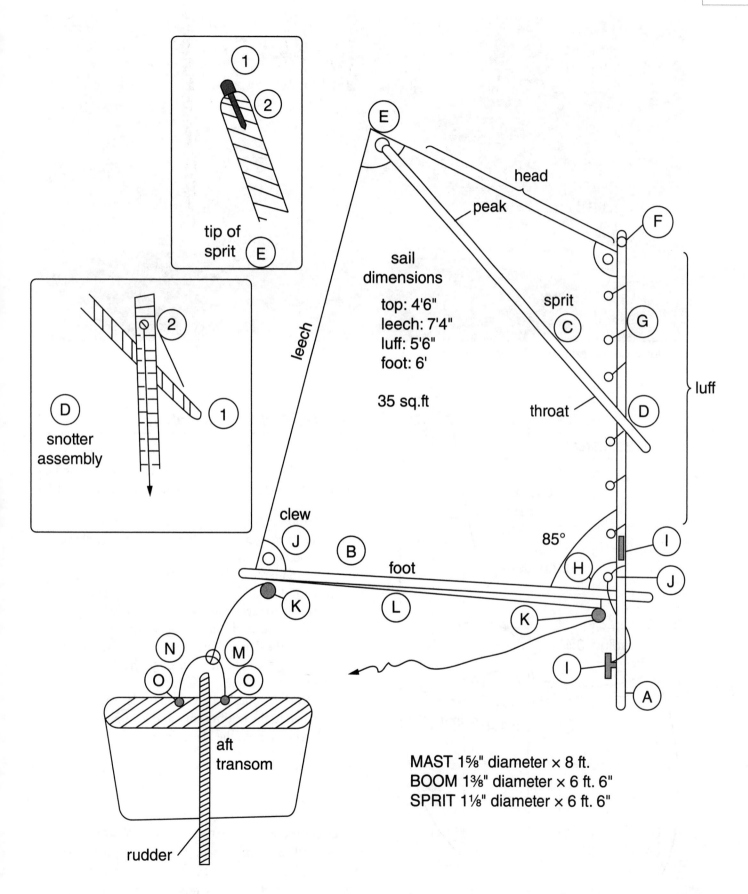

tip of
sprit

snotter
assembly

head

peak

sprit

throat

leech

sail
dimensions

top: 4'6"
leech: 7'4"
luff: 5'6"
foot: 6'

35 sq.ft

luff

clew

foot

85°

aft
transom

rudder

MAST 1⅝" diameter × 8 ft.
BOOM 1⅜" diameter × 6 ft. 6"
SPRIT 1⅛" diameter × 6 ft. 6"

The Uqbar on the left shows the kick-up rudder.

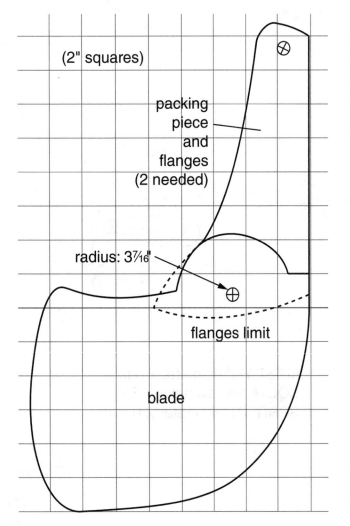

(2" squares)

packing
piece
and
flanges
(2 needed)

radius: 3⁷⁄₁₆"

flanges limit

blade

Kick-Up Rudder (All Uqbars)

The rudder consists of two flanges, a packing piece, and the blade. (The packing piece and the blade have to be of the same thickness, ½" plywood or ⅛" aluminum.)

Instructions
1. Trace packing piece and blade on the same sheet of plywood or aluminum. Cut.
2. Cut two identical flanges by tracing the packing piece and extending the flanges as per plan.
3. Laminate the two flanges with the packing piece.
   When cured, insert the blade into the space between the flanges. Drill the hole for the pivot (a ⅜" carriage bolt, bronze) through the flanges and blade.
   Note: if yours is a plywood blade, a shock cord attached to the leading edge and led up to the tiller will serve to hold the blade down in the water.

An Uqbar rudder can be made of either plywood or aluminum. If plywood is used, then a shock cord of some type must be used to hold the rudder down in the water, since it would otherwise tend to float to the surface.

How Good an Eye Do You Have?

Can you spot the visual flaw in this Uqbar? There is a reverse curve of the sheer aft of the bow transom. This does not detract from the dinghy's maritime quality, but is a bit jarring to the eye. If after gluing the hull such a reverse curvature materializes, just push the sides apart and insert the forward seat or a batten to maintain the spacing. It will maintain its shape after the forward seat, the rubrail, and the inwale are installed. (Courtesy Bill Joseph)

Uqbar 7
Superlight Yacht Tender
Row/Sail/Motor

Chapter Contents

Description/Specifications

LOA (LENGTH) 6'10"
BEAM (WIDTH) 48"
DRAFT 25" WITH DAGGERBOARD DOWN
WEIGHT 42 LBS.
CAPACITY 2+ ADULTS

Here is a yacht tender that can carry up to three persons in calm waters yet is compact enough to fit aboard most powerboats or sailing yachts. Uqbar 7 is 6'10" long, 48" wide, and weighs 42 lbs. She can be hoisted aboard or handled onshore single-handedly, yet she moves very nimbly under oars or a small outboard (2 hp recommended).

The author rowing an Uqbar 7.

The aft seat is cut back at the sides to allow more legroom, and the center seat features a bulge (a rounded extension—see diagram of seat supports for Uqbar 7 on page 36) on the forward side so that the rower can shift weight for better trim according to the load. Uqbar 7 is fun to sail and moves right along with her sprit rig, kick-up rudder, and single clip-on leeboard with kick-up blade.

She is without doubt one of the most handsome, practical, and affordable yacht tenders in existence.

Building Materials and Other Supplies

Wood

Plywood

___ 2 sheets 4' × 8' ¼" top-grade Luan, marine, or exterior good two sides

___ ½ sheet (i.e., 4' × 4') ⅜" plywood

Laminate double thickness of the ¼" stock where ½" is indicated.

Pine

___ 1½" × ¾" × 7', 4 pieces (seat risers)

___ ¾" × 1½" × 3', 1 piece

___ 1 plank ¾" × 4" × 24" (forward seat riser/pad for eyebolt)

Ash

___ 4 strips ⅝" × 1" × 86" (for rubrails and inwales)

___ 1 plank ¾" × 3" × 32" (for the skeg)

Sailboats Only

___ Ash: 1" × 1¼" × 48" (for tiller and tiller cheeks)

___ Clothes-hanger stock (i.e., dowel rods such as one might use in a closet) for spars:

  ___ 1⅝" diameter × 8' (for the mast)

  ___ 1⅜" diameter × 6'6" (for the boom)

  ___ 1⅛" diameter × 6'6" (for the sprit)

Fasteners

___ Bare copper wire, #4, 7-strand, 6' (yields over 100 wire-ties); obtain from your favorite electrical supply or local hardware store

___ **OR** round plastic wire-tires (100 needed)

___ 2 galvanized lag bolts, ¼" × 1½", with oversize washers

___ Various temporary wood screws, #8 × 1" and 1¼"

An Uqbar 7 under sail. Note clip-on leeboard on starboard.

Epoxy Products

___ WEST SYSTEM epoxy products (available in many building supplies stores) or other brand. (Note: always use mask and protective gloves.)

___ 3 quarts epoxy resin plus hardener (rowing models: 2 quarts)

___ Fiberglass tape: 2" or 3" wide × 30'

___ 8 oz. microfibers

___ 5 oz. filleting blend or microballoons

___ 1 oz. colloidal silica (optional)

___ 6 dozen disposable brushes or similar

___ 6 pairs disposable sponge roller sleeves

___ 6 small plastic squeegees

Hardware and Miscellaneous

All Models

___ 2 pairs oarlocks

___ 1 galvanized eyebolt ⅜" × 2" (also called a tow-eye)

Sailboats Only
___ 1 bronze screw #12 × 3" (for head of the sprit)
___ 2 bronze carriage bolts, ⅜" × 3" and ⅜" × 2" (for rudder blade and tiller pivots)
___ 1 bronze carriage bolt, ⅜" × 3" (for leeboard pivot)
___ 2 pairs pintles and gudgeons with appropriate bolts and finishing washers (stainless steel or bronze)
___ 2 small blocks and 3 small cleats (for ¼" line)
___ 20' of ⅛" lacing line and 36' of ¼" Dacron line
___ SAIL: 32 sq. ft., 3 or 3.5 oz. Dacron (obtain from your local sailmaker or the Internet, or make it yourself)

Building Uqbar 7

The step-by-step instructions on pages 58–76 are used for building the whole Uqbar series. Since they were written specifically for Uqbar 8, however, there are differences in dimensions, and also in some details.

To build Uqbar 7, then, just follow the instructions on pages 58–76, but incorporate the variants below for the relevant sections. Note that the sail rig and rudder are the same as for U8. (See pages 26–28.)

Gluing on the Keelson

As a spreader, use the center seat, inserted so that its aft edge is 32" forward of the transom, as measured straight from the top of the transom seat support.

Installing the Seats

1. The center seat is already in place, although without its support.
2. The aft and forward seats were cut slightly oversize. Trim and fit by shaving off equal amounts on both sides, keeping the proper bevel. Knock off the corners of the aft seat to accommodate the fillet.
3. Assemble the center seat support by snapping the two parts into each other at a right angle. Epoxy the assembly. Let cure. (Placing it over a mild heat source will speed up the process.)
4. Check all supports so that they fit snugly into position. The aft and forward seat supports are vertical to the baseline, not the bottom: place the boat on a level surface, resting on its skeg, and use a level or a plumb line. Trim the supports as needed.
5. Epoxy the seats in position, holding them in place with a few screws or clamps.
6. Generously coat with thick epoxy the top and lower edges of the supports, and push into position. If you trimmed them to a tight fit, they'll stay there firmly. If a little loose, hold in position with whatever means, such as tape or a few partially driven-in nails.
7. Make small fillets in the angles formed by the junction of the supports/keelson and supports/seats.

   Note: if you do not mind the added weight, you may laminate two pieces of ¼" plywood for the seats instead of using ⅜" plywood.

Sailing Models
Mast Step

The mast step is glued to the keelson and the forward seat support. It is placed under the seat, forward of the support. First drill through the seat for the mast, 1½" forward of the seat's edge. Then, making sure that the mast is vertical, determine the exact place for the step, and glue.

Sailing Rig and Rudder

Same as for Uqbar 8—see pages 27–28.

Instead of a daggerboard and trunk, Uqbar 7 uses a single clip-on leeboard.

Leeboard Assembly

1. The kick-up leeboard consists of two parts: the head, which hooks over the rubrail, and the kick-up blade itself.
2. The head: The hook is separated from the head proper by two wooden spacer blocks of the same thickness as the gunwale (i.e., the rubrail + hull material + inwale), normally 1¼". Glue the blocks on the head as indicated. After it cures, center the hook, placed on its straight edge, and drill two ¼" holes in continuation of those predrilled in the hook. You will then assemble and glue using the carriage bolts provided, heads outside. Do *not* assemble until you have threaded through the ⅜" carriage bolt that serves as the blade pivot.
3. The blade: Glue the handle on the blade as indicated. After it cures, drill a ⅜" hole through the handle, blade, and head, as indicated on the plans. Then thread the carriage bolt, glue and bolt the hook, and you're in business.

Leeboard Installation

1. Push the assembled head over the rail so that the hook is just aft of the center seat, touching it, and the lower block sits on the gunwale. This is its correct permanent position. Now you can glue on the inside right of the inwale the two wooden blocks that serve to hold the hook in position.

Scale: ⅜" = 1"

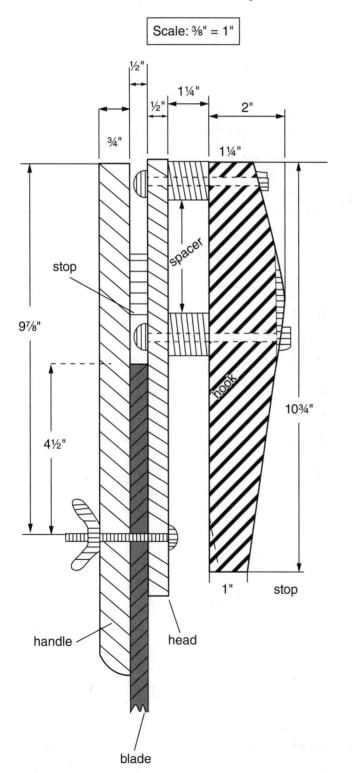

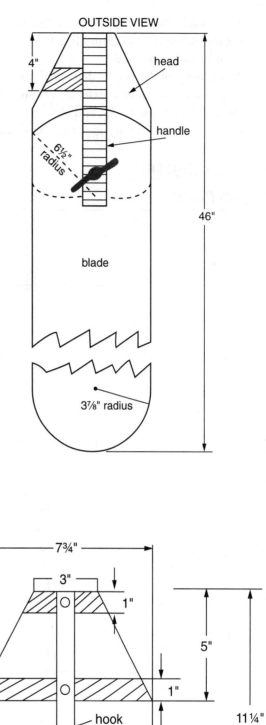

Plans for the clip-on leeboard with kick-up blade.

(But see #2, below.) A lanyard through a hole in the hook should be used to ensure that the leeboard cannot be lost overboard.

2. Before gluing on the blocks, determine the side of the boat on which you prefer to mount the leeboard. Glue these blocks, and also the stop, on the proper side on the outside of the head. This stop is aft of the handle. Its function is to prevent the blade from swiveling forward of the vertical, while leaving it free to swing back should an obstacle be struck. A shock cord attached to the top of the handle and led back to any convenient point will help hold it in position, while allowing the blade to swing back.

Cutting Diagrams

Bottom Plank

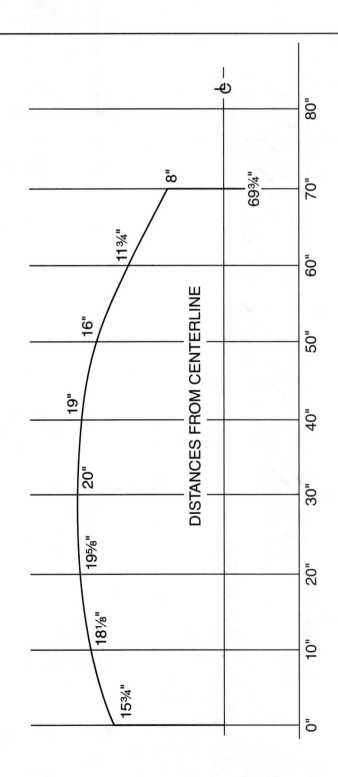

Side Plank (2 needed)

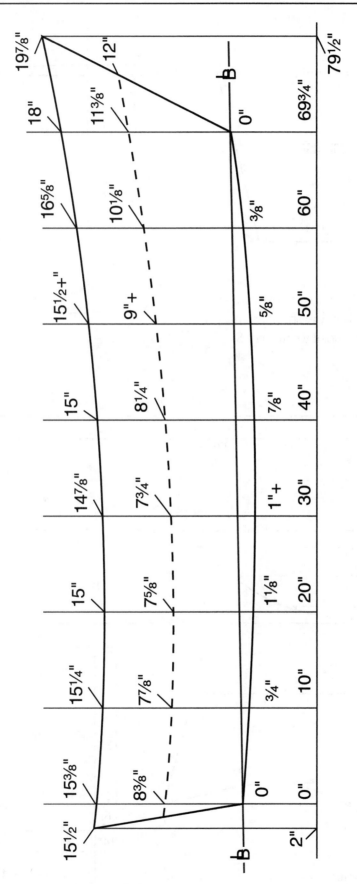

Transoms

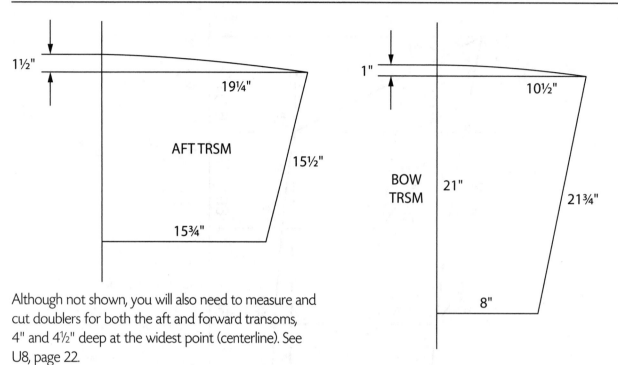

Although not shown, you will also need to measure and cut doublers for both the aft and forward transoms, 4" and 4½" deep at the widest point (centerline). See U8, page 22.

Seats

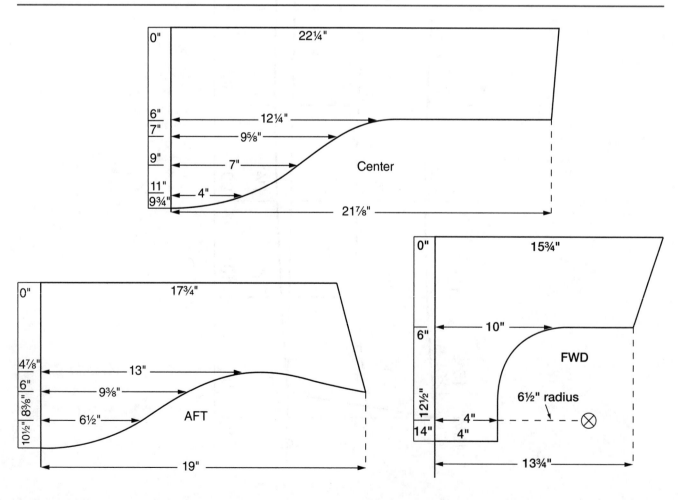

Seat Supports

(Grid: 1" squares)

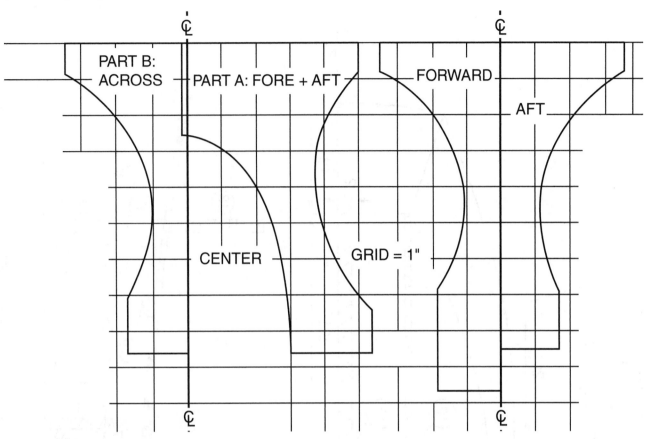

Plans and Key to Plans

Key to Profile and Half-Breadth (See page 38.)

1. Transom doublers, ½" plywood (¾" aft if outboard is used).
2. Tow-eye, ⅜" × 2½" shoulder eyebolt, galvanized.
3. Forward seat riser, ¾" × 4" pine, beveled 55 degrees on top.
4. Side plank seat riser, ½" × ¾" pine, beveled 10 degrees on top.
5. Forward seat, ⅜" plywood.
6. Forward seat support, ⅜" plywood.
7. Center seat, ⅜" plywood.
8. Center seat support, ⅜" plywood.
9. Aft seat, ⅜" plywood.
10. Aft seat support, ⅜" plywood.
11. Lag bolts and oversize washers, ¼" × 1½", galvanized.
12. Skeg, ¾" × 3" × 32" ash or oak.
13. Ash rubrails outside, inwales inside, ½" × ¾".
14. Oarlock pads, ½" plywood.
15. Keelson, ¼" × 4" plywood.
16. Bottom runners, ½" × ¾" pine.
17. Two-piece mast step, ¾" × 4" pine.
18. Mast, 1⅝" diameter.
19. Rudder (see page 28).
20. Tiller and tiller cheeks, ¾" × 1½" ash.
21. Tiller pivot, ⅜" × 2½" carriage bolt, bronze.
22. Pad for lower gudgeon, ½" × 2" × 4" (sailboats only).

Half-Breadth and Profile

(See illustration key, page 37.)

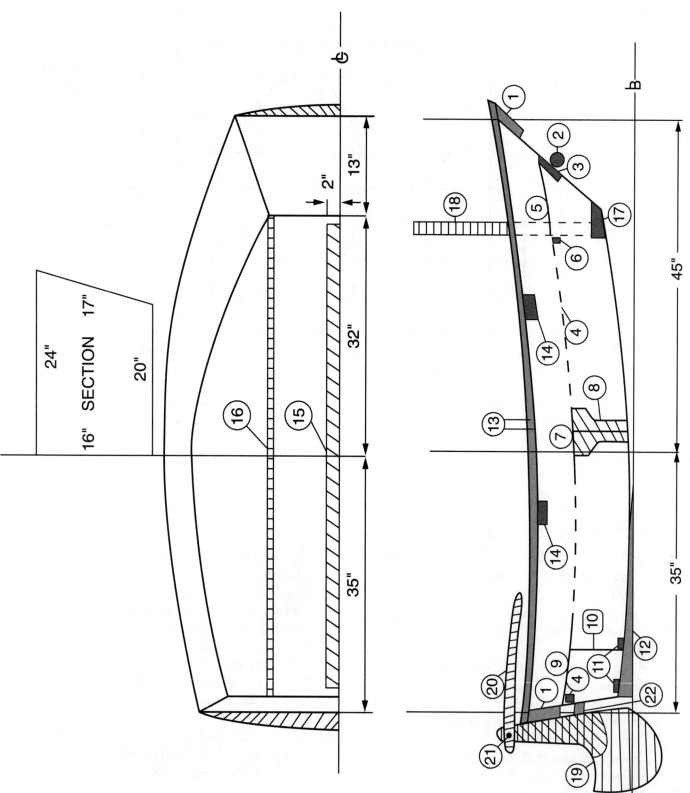

Seat Supports

The aft and forward supports are installed athwartships, the foot on the keelson and the top set back ½" from the seat's edge.

The center seat support is assembled by sliding parts A and B into each other, and then epoxying the assembly. (See illustration on page 53, bottom left, as an example.)

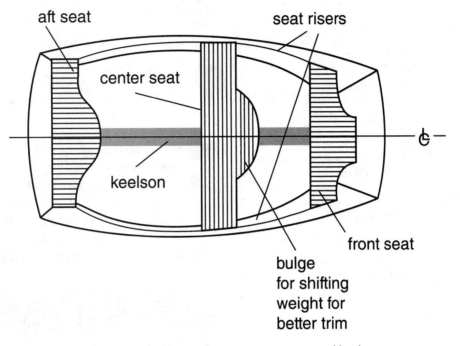

A plan view of Uqbar 7 showing seats, risers, and keelson.

An Uqbar 7 with sailing rig and kickup leeboard.

Uqbar 10
The All-Purpose Skiff
Row/Sail/Motor

scale: ⅛" = 1"

Chapter Contents

Description/Specifications

LOA (LENGTH) 9'10"
BEAM (WIDTH) 49"
DRAFT 34" WITH DAGGERBOARD DOWN
WEIGHT 72 LBS.
CAPACITY 4+ ADULTS

The success of Uqbar 8 led to her big brother, a 10-foot pram-nosed dinghy built according to the same principles and with the same general lines.

Uqbar 10's hull is of ¼" fir marine plywood, and transoms and seats are of the same plywood or top-grade Luan. This is because Luan is not generally available as a 4' × 10' panel, as needed here.

Rowing an Uqbar dinghy is delightful: light and small, they move quickly across any body of water.

An Uqbar 10 under sail.

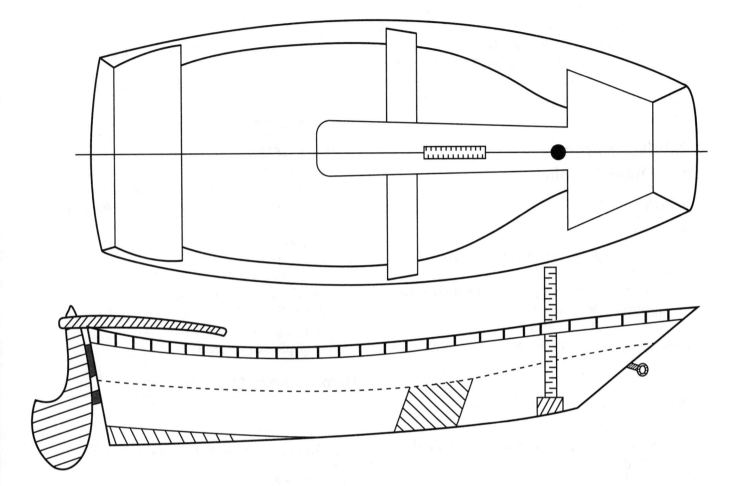

U10 seat arrangement showing a fore-and-aft seat.

Uqbar 10 is 9'10" long, 49" wide, and weighs only 72 pounds. She is easily car-topped, and is mainly used as a primary boat for traveling on the water, fishing, gunkholing, or just plain enjoyment under oars, sail, or motor.

She is a good sailer, easy to handle and very stable. Her sailing equipment includes a sprit rig, an efficient daggerboard, and a kick-up rudder. Watch her go to windward with four persons aboard!

Gunkholing with U10. This one was built in 1983 and is still going strong.

Building Uqbar 10

Please go to "Building Uqbar," page 58.

The same step-by-step instructions are used for building the entire Uqbar series. Since they were written specifically for Uqbar 8, however, there are differences in dimensions and also in some details. So, to build Uqbar 10, follow the instructions on pages 58–76, but incorporate the size differences as per the U10 plans. Note that the kick-up rudder is the same as that for U8. (See page 28.)

Building Materials and Other Supplies

Wood

Plywood

___1 sheet 4' × 10'1⁄4" marine or exterior plywood good two sides

___1½ sheets 4' × 8' same plywood or top-grade Luan (rowing model: 1 sheet)

___3⁄8" plywood: 1 sheet 4' × 8'

Laminate double thickness where ½" is indicated.

Pine

___2 pieces 10' × 3⁄4" × 1", 2 pieces 8' (for the seat risers)

___3⁄4" × 1½": 20'

___1 plank 3⁄4" × 4" × 24" (forward seat riser/pad for eyebolt)

Ash

___4 strips 5⁄8" × 1" × 8' (for rubrails and inwales)

___1 plank 3⁄4" × 5" × 48" (for the skeg)

Sailboats Only

___Ash: 1" × 1¼" × 48" (tiller and tiller cheeks)

___Clothes-hanger stock (i.e., dowel rods of fir or pine such as one might use in a closet) for spars:

   ___1⅝" diameter × 10' (for the mast)

   ___1⅜" diameter × 8' (for the boom)

   ___1⅛" diameter × 8' (for the sprit)

Fasteners

___Bare copper wire, #4, 7-strand, 6' (yields over 100 wire-ties); obtain from your favorite electrical supply or local hardware store

___**OR** round plastic wire-tires (100 needed)

___2 galvanized lag bolts, ¼" × 1½", with oversize washers

___Various temporary wood screws, #8 × 1" and 1¼"

Epoxy Products

___WEST SYSTEM epoxy products (available in many building supplies stores) or other brand. (Note: always use mask and protective gloves.)

___3 quarts epoxy resin plus hardener (rowing models: 2 quarts)

___Fiberglass tape: 2" or 3" wide × 30'

___8 oz. microfibers

___5 oz. filleting blend or microballoons

___1 oz. colloidal silica (optional)

___6 dozen disposable acid brushes or similar

___6 pairs disposable sponge roller sleeves

___6 small plastic squeegees

Hardware and Miscellaneous

All Models

___2 pairs oarlocks

___1 galvanized eyebolt 3⁄8" × 2" (a so-called tow-eye)

Sailboats Only

___1 bronze screw #12 × 3" (for head of the sprit)

___2 bronze carriage bolts, 3⁄8" × 3" and 3⁄8" × 2" (for rudder blade and tiller pivots)

___1 bronze carriage bolt 3⁄8" × 3" (for leeboard pivot)

___2 pairs pintles and gudgeons with appropriate bolts and finishing washers (stainless steel or bronze)

___2 small blocks and 3 small cleats (for ¼" line)

___20' of ⅛" lacing line and 36' of ¼" Dacron line

___SAIL: 52 sq. ft., 3 or 3.5 oz. Dacron (from your local sailmaker, or request quotes on the Internet, or sew your own)

Cutting Diagrams

Bottom Plank

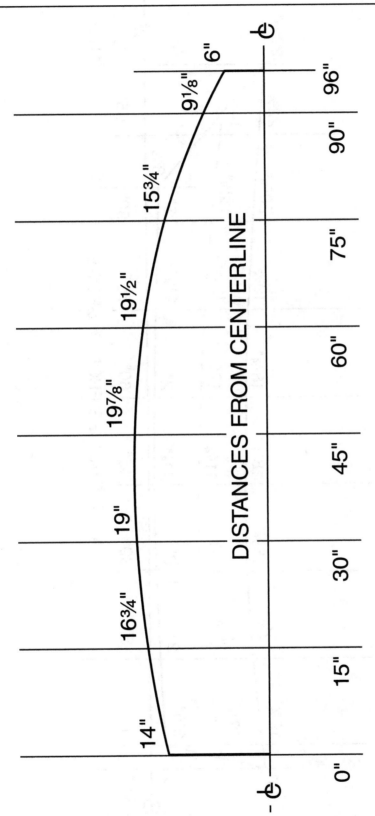

Side Plank

(2 needed)

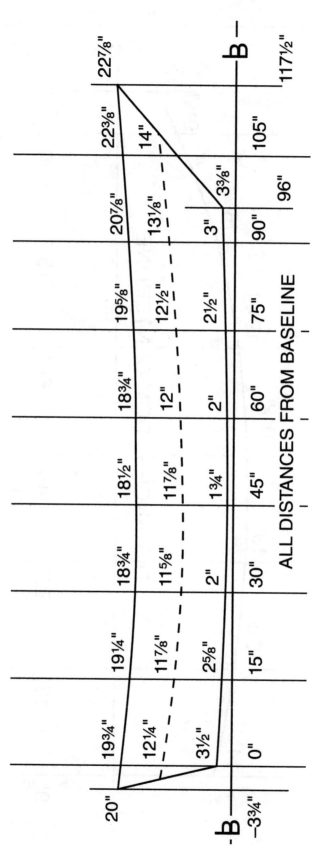

Both cut from the 4' × 10' sheet.

Transoms

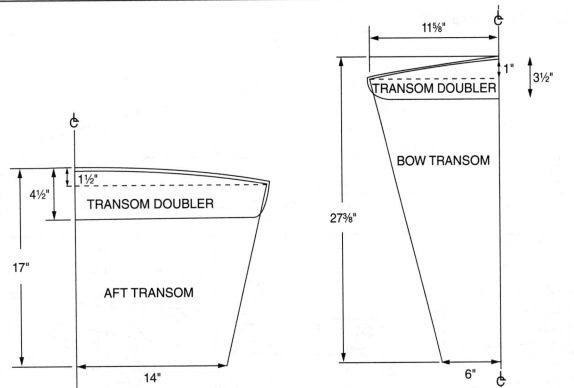

Seats and King Plank

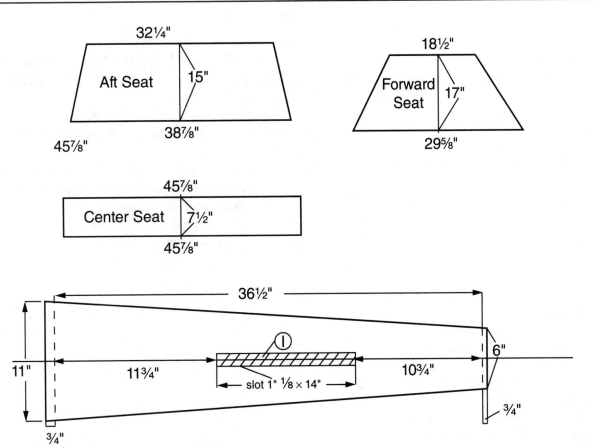

Plans and Key to Plans

Profile and Half-Breadth

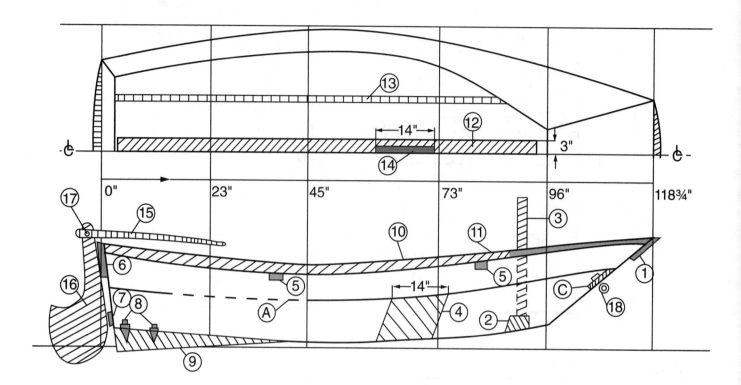

Key to Profile and Half-Breadth

1. Bow transom doubler, ½" plywood.
2. Mast step 2½" × 3½" × 5" pine, with 1⅝"-diameter hole.
3. Mast.
4. Daggerboard trunk.
5. Oarlock pads, ½" plywood.
6. Aft transom doubler, ½" plywood.
7. Lower gudgeon pad, ½" plywood.
8. Galvanized lag bolts, ¼" × 1½", with oversize washers.
9. Skeg, ¾" × 5" × 48" ash or oak.
10. Rubrails, outside, ⅝" × 1" ash.
11. Inwales, ½" × 1" ash.
12. Keelson, ¼" plywood.
13. Bottom runners, ¾" × 1" pine.
14. Slot for daggerboard trunk.
15. Tiller, ash.
16. Rudder, ½" plywood. See also kick-up rudder option on page 28.
17. Tiller pivot, bronze carriage bolt, ⅜".
18. Tow-eye, ⁵⁄₁₆" or ⅜" galvanized eyebolt.

Key to Seats and King Plank at Seat-Riser Level

A. Side seat risers, ¾" × 1" × 107½", beveled 18 degrees on top.
B. Aft seat riser, same stock as A.
C. Forward seat riser, ¾" × 5", beveled 45 degrees on top.
D, E, and F. Seat supports, ¾" × 1½", double-beveled and notched at each end to fit around seat risers.
G. King plank and doubler.
H. Mast partner, 1⅝" hole through king plank combo.
I. Slot for daggerboard trunk, 14" × 1⅛".

Seats and King Plank at Seat-Riser Level

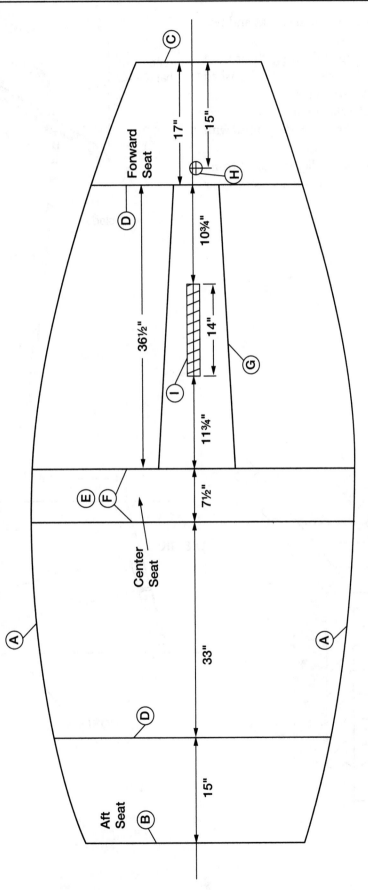

Daggerboard and Trunk

The trunk is made of two ¼" plywood cheeks and two
⅝" × ¾" posts. The slot is ⅝" wide.

The stop is glued to the top of the daggerboard and
reinforced with a few brass screws (#6 × 1½") pushed
into oversize pilot holes filled with epoxy.

The handle consists of a short length of ¼" rope,
the ends pushed into oversize holes 1½" deep, filled with
epoxy.

Reminder: if desired, instead of daggerboard + trunk
+ king plank, you may opt to use a clip-on leeboard as for
U7. (See page 33.)

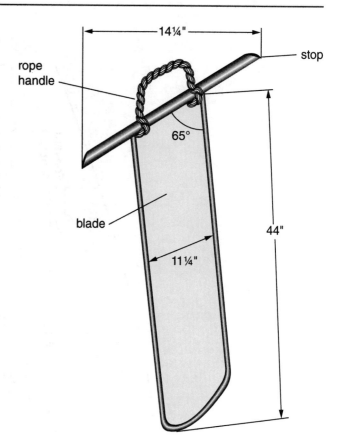

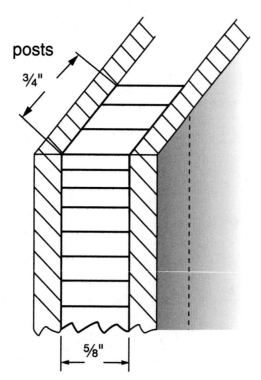

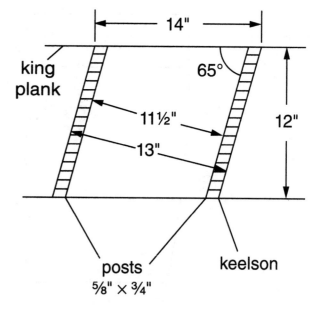

Sailing Rig

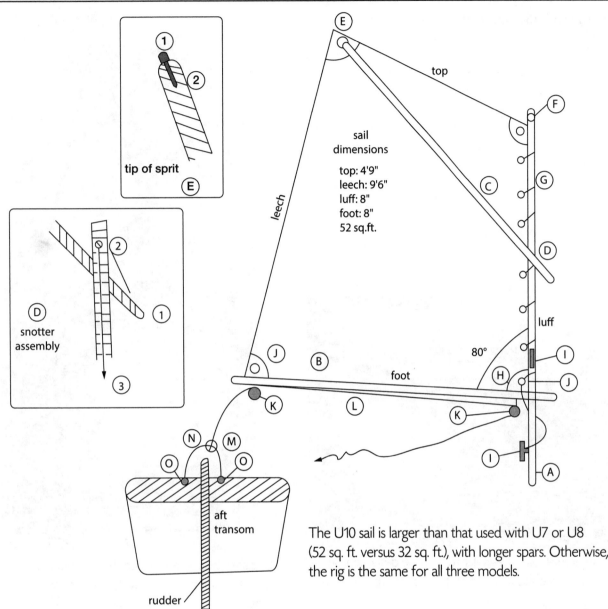

tip of sprit

snotter assembly

top

sail dimensions

top: 4'9"
leech: 9'6"
luff: 8"
foot: 8"
52 sq.ft.

leech

luff

80°

foot

aft transom

rudder

The U10 sail is larger than that used with U7 or U8 (52 sq. ft. versus 32 sq. ft.), with longer spars. Otherwise, the rig is the same for all three models.

Key to Sailing Rig

A. Mast, 1⅝" diameter × 10'.

B. Boom, 1⅜" diameter × 9'.

C. Sprit, 1⅛" diameter × 8'.

D. Snotter assembly: The control line is dead-ended at 1, goes through a hole in the mast at 2, thence to cleat I on mast (3) (or on deck).

E. Tip of sprit: A large bronze screw (#12 × 2½"), top cut off and rounded (1), is pushed into an oversize pilot hole filled with epoxy (2).

F and G. The sail is permanently bent to the mast with a lacing line dead-ended through the hole at F, and laced down.

H. The downhaul goes around the mast once and down to cleat I.

I. Cleats for downhaul and for snotter.

J. Clew and tack are laced to boom. The sail is otherwise loose-footed.

K. Blocks: As light as possible, since your head will be close by!

L. The sheet is dead-ended at M to a ring around the rope traveler (or a simple bowline), thence revved through blocks K and back into the sailor's hand.

M. Ring, brass (or bowline).

N. Rope traveler.

O. The rope traveler is dead-ended through holes at O with figure-8 knots.

Rudder

The rudder is the same as that for U8. (See page 28.)

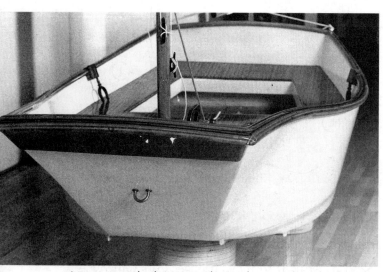

An amateur-built U10 similar to the one described on page 46. Note the tow eye on the bow transom.

A U10 standing on end. Note the laminated seats and side seat additions, plus a divider on the forward seat. Handsome, but not terribly useful.

Uqbar 6
Le Mini-Tender
Row/Motor

Chapter Contents

Description/Specifications

LOA (LENGTH) 5'11"
BEAM (WIDTH) 46"
DRAFT 15"
WEIGHT 35 LBS.
CAPACITY 2+ ADULTS

The latest addition to the Uqbar clan of prams, Le Mini-Tender is a carry-aboard yacht tender that weighs only 35 pounds and easily takes two adults plus gear. It is 5'11" long, 46" wide, and 15" deep, and is usually fitted aboard the mothership athwartships on the cabintop, under the boom.

Le Mini-Tender is exceptionally roomy for her size. There is no middle thwart to restrict legroom; instead, a continuous rowing station/combo allows the proper distribution of weight.

Like all Uqbars, Le Mini-Tender is built of top-grade Luan or other plywood, ash, and WEST SYSTEM epoxy products. It can be finished bright and strikes a distinctive figure with its seakindly rounded forefoot, flaring bows, arc bottom, and moderate rocker. The U6 is a far cry from the slab-sided prams of yore!

An Uqbar 6 mini-tender tied up on a rocky shore.

Building Materials and Other Supplies

Wood

Plywood

___¼" Luan, marine, or exterior good two sides: 2½ sheets 4' × 8'

Laminate double thickness where ½" is indicated.

Pine

___Parting strips ½" × ¾" × 6': 4 pieces
___1 plank ¾" × 4" × 18" (for the forward seat riser and pad for eyebolt)

Ash

___4 strips ½" × ¾" × 6' (for the rubrails and inwales)
___1 plank ¾" × 3" × 24" (for the skeg)

Fasteners

___Bare copper wire, #4, 7-strand, 6' (yields over 100 wire-ties); obtain from your favorite electrical supply or local hardware store
___**OR** round plastic wire-tires (100 needed)
___2 galvanized lag bolts ¼" × 1½", with oversize washers
___Various temporary wood screws #8 × 1" and 1¼"

Epoxy Products

___WEST SYSTEM epoxy products (available in many building supplies stores) or other brand. (Note: always use mask and protective gloves.)
___2 quarts epoxy resin plus hardener
___Fiberglass tape: 2" or 3" wide × 20'
___8 oz. microfibers
___5 oz. filleting blend or microballoons
___1 oz. colloidal silica (optional)
___6 dozen disposable acid brushes, useful for spreading epoxy of various thicknesses
___6 pairs disposable sponge roller sleeves
___6 small plastic squeegees

Hardware and Miscellaneous

___2 pairs oarlocks
___1 galvanized eyebolt ⅜" × 2" (a so-called tow-eye)

Note: U6 is not recommended as a sailboat except in very restricted waters.

Building Uqbar 6

The same step-by-step instructions are used for building the whole Uqbar series. Since they were written specifically for Uqbar 8, however, there are differences in dimensions, and also in some details and procedures.

So, to build Uqbar 6, just follow the instructions for building U8 (pages 58–76), but incorporate the variants noted below for the relevant sections.

Assembling the Hull

The aft end is raised level 2" and the forward end 2½".

Gluing on the Keelson

1. As a spreader, use a temporary batten ¾" × 1½" × 40" beveled and notched to fit around and under the side seat risers. This batten is inserted 31" forward of the transom, as measured from just above the aft seat riser. *This spreader is to remain in place until you have glued on inwales, rubrails, and knees.* It is then discarded.

2. At the same time you're gluing on the keelson, you can glue on the *panting beam* and packing pieces. Trace a line across the bottom, 30" forward of the aft edge, and center the pieces on that line. The packing pieces are on both sides of the keelson, with a ½" space in between as a *limber hole.* The panting beam is then exactly superimposed. The assembly is short about ½" on the port and starboard sides to allow space for the epoxy fillet. Just coat the pieces with gluing epoxy, place, and hold in position with some weights.

   Before proceeding, it is necessary to glue on the inwales, which are full length. Continue with the following two sections, "Installing the Inwales" and "Installing the Knees," respectively; then go on to "Installing the Seats."

Installing the Inwales

1. Notch the top corners, port and starboard, of the bow and aft transoms ½" × ¾", to receive the inwales. The inwales are clamped inside of the side planks, flush with the top and protruding slightly forward and aft.
2. Make sure the inwales fit well, and remove.
3. Prepare gluing epoxy, coat the matching surfaces, and glue on. Hold the pieces with small clamps or

temporary screws. (Pilot holes will be needed in the hard wood.)

4. After cure, snip off the inwales flush with the outside face of the transoms.

Installing the Knees

1. The knees can be installed at the same time as the inwales. They are placed, centered, on the line previously traced 30" forward of the bottom plank's aft edge. They should fit snugly against the side plank and the panting beam, and flush against the underside of the seat riser.
2. Saturate the end grain thoroughly with coating epoxy, then glue on with thick gluing epoxy. If you managed a tight fit, the knees will hold in place by themselves. If not, use small nails partially *toed in*.
3. Prepare a small amount of filleting epoxy, and fillet all seams.
4. Reinforce by pushing small lengths of fiberglass tape into the wet fillet, the same way you did at the forefoot. Let cure.

Installing the Seats

Since you have already installed the knees, you may re-move the temporary spreader if it is in the way.

1. Assemble the T-shaped rowing station support by coating its two parts with epoxy, snapping them into each other, and filleting the assembly. If needed, cure under a lightbulb to speed up the process.
2. Assemble the forward seat and the rowing station/king plank combo.

   Trace a centerline on both parts.

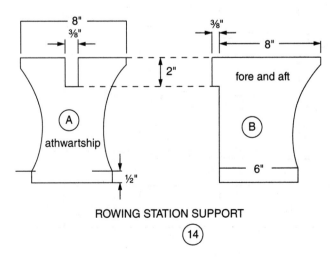

ROWING STATION SUPPORT

(14)

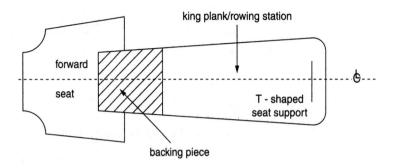

Lay the parts down flat on a piece of plastic sheeting, underside up, so that they are pushed against each other and the centerlines form one continuous line.

Make sure the backing piece is exactly centered on the seam.

Separate, apply gluing epoxy, and glue, hold-ing down the backing piece in position with some weights.

3. Fit the aft seat into position. You may have to shave it equally on both sides, keeping the proper bevel, until a snug fit is achieved. Note that the aft corners are notched to fit around the epoxy fillet.
4. Dry-fit it, using screws (#8 × 1", countersunk) and/or clamps.
5. Push the seat support into position, centered on the keelson, so that it is set back about 1½" from the seat's forward edge. Shave if necessary. It should be a tight fit.
6. Do the same for the rowing station/forward seat combo, making sure it is centered. (Let the rowing station part flop down at this point.) After the seat is secured in place, push up the rowing station part, and insert the support. The bottom of the aft edge should be just about level with the seat risers on both sides. Trim if need be.
7. Insert the two other supports. These also should fit tightly.
8. Now remove everything.
9. Thoroughly saturate all end grain with coating epoxy.
10. Thicken your mix for gluing, and glue the aft and forward seats in position.
11. Now coat the top and bottom edges of the support with gluing epoxy, and push into position. The supports will hold position by themselves if the fit is tight. If not, use temporary nails or tape.
12. Fillet all seams, and push small lengths of fiberglass tape into the seams as reinforcements.

Installing Oarlock Pads and Oarlocks

Note: the inwales are already in position. There are two rowing positions and two sets of oarlock pads.

1. The oarlock pads are installed under and flush against the inwales.
2. Measure about 9" aft from the aft edge of the rowing station, and mark on the inwales.
3. Measure 10" to 11" aft of the aft edge of the forward seat proper, and mark on the inwales.
4. Coat the pads with gluing epoxy, center on your marks, and glue on, holding the pads in position with clamps.

Cutting Diagrams

Bottom Plank

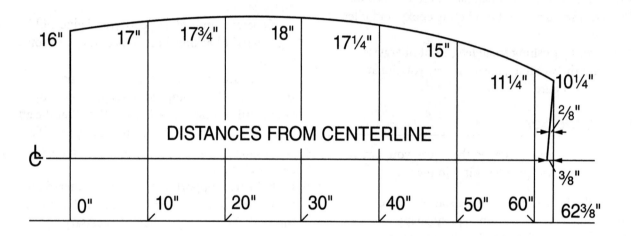

Side Plank (2 needed)

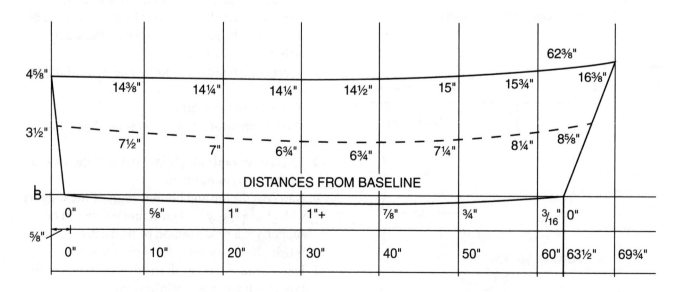

Transoms and Supports

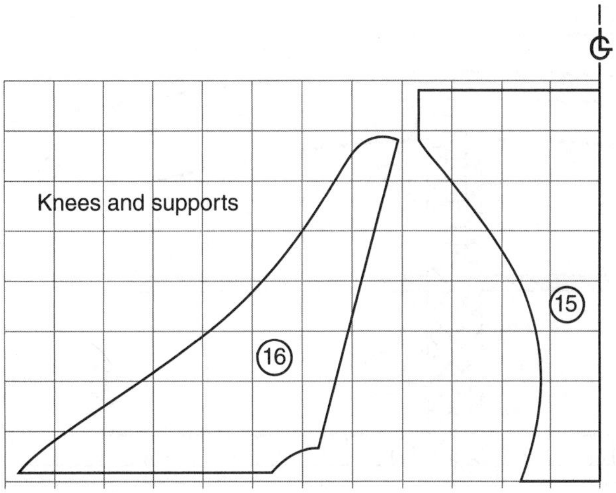
CL
Knees and supports
16
15

scale: 1" grid

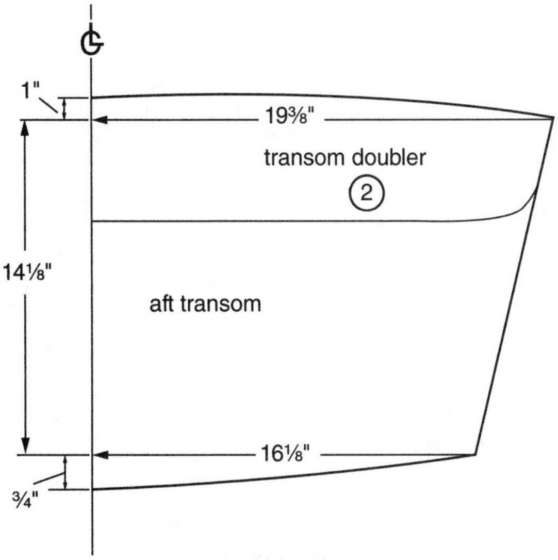
CL
1"
19 3/8"
transom doubler
2
14 1/8"
aft transom
16 1/8"
3/4"

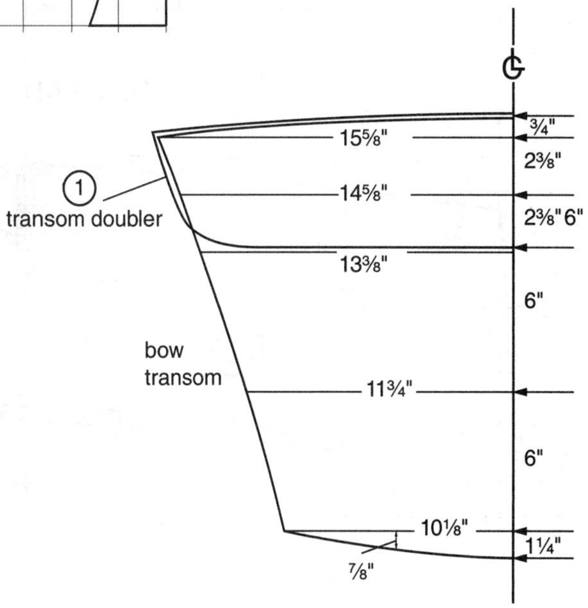
CL
3/4"
15 5/8"
2 3/8"
1
transom doubler
14 5/8"
2 3/8" 6"
13 3/8"
6"
bow
transom
11 3/4"
6"
10 1/8"
1 1/4"
7/8"

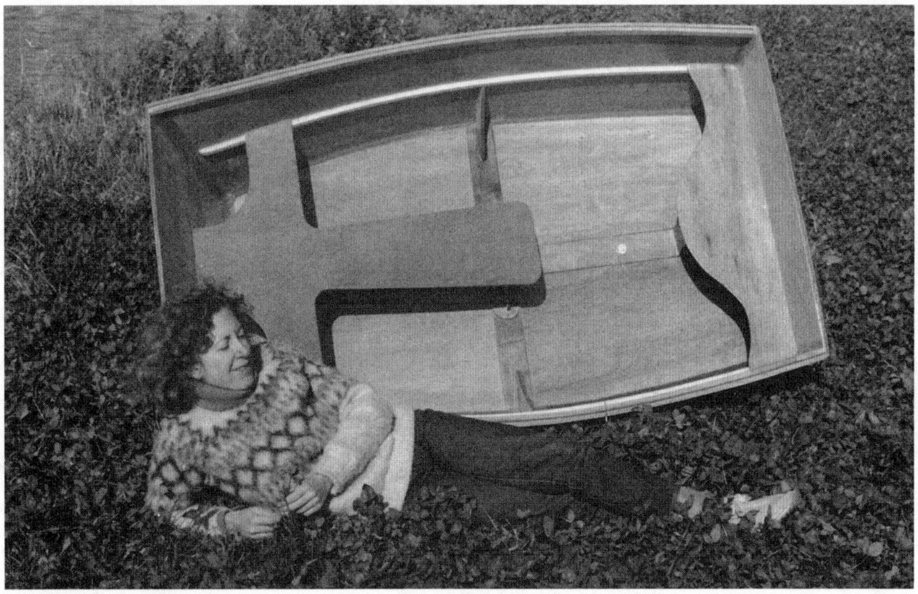

Plans and Key to Plans

Profile and Half-Breadth

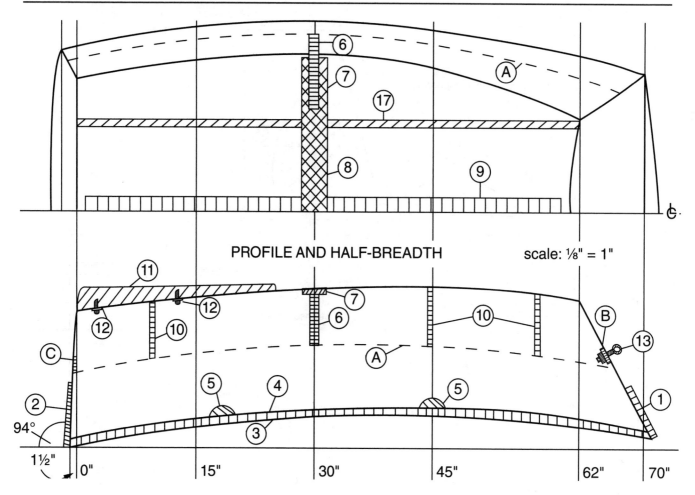

PROFILE AND HALF-BREADTH

scale: ⅛" = 1"

94°

1½"

0"   15"   30"   45"   62"   70"

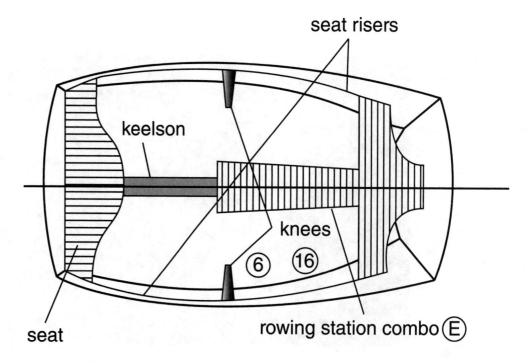

seat risers

keelson

knees

⑥ ⑯

seat

rowing station combo Ⓔ

Key to Plans and Cutting Diagrams
(see pages 55 and 56)

1. Bow transom doubler, ⅜" or ½" plywood.
2. Aft transom doubler, ½" plywood.
3. Rubrail outside, ¾" × ⅝" × 6'. Two needed.
4. Inwale inside, ¾" × ½" × 6'. Two needed.
5. Oarlock pads, ½" plywood. Four needed.
6. Knee, ½" plywood (see also #16). Two needed.
7. Panting beam, ⅜" (or ½") × 3½" plywood.
8. Packing pieces, ¼" × 3½" plywood. Two needed.
9. Keelson, ¼" × 3½" × 6' plywood.
10. Seat supports, ⅜" (or ½") plywood. (Also see #15.) Three needed.
11. Skeg, ¾" × 3" × 24" ash or oak.
12. Galvanized lag bolts, ¼" × 1½", plus oversize washers. Two needed.
13. Tow-eye, 5/16" × 2" galvanized shoulder eye-bolt.
14. Rowing station support, half profile, page 53, ⅜" plywood (or ½").
15. Seat supports, half profile, page 55, (also see #10). Three needed.
16. Knee (see #6). Two needed.
17. Bottom runners, ¾" × ½" × 66" parting strip, pine. Two needed.

A. Seat riser, ¾" × ½" pine parting strip, beveled 15 degrees on top. Two needed.
B. Forward seat riser, pine. ¾" × 4" × 4", beveled 50 degrees.
C. Aft seat riser, ¾" × 1½", pine, beveled 10 degrees on top.
D. Aft seat, ⅜" or ½" plywood.
E. Rowing station/forward seat combo, ⅜" or ½" plywood.

Seats at Seat-Riser Level

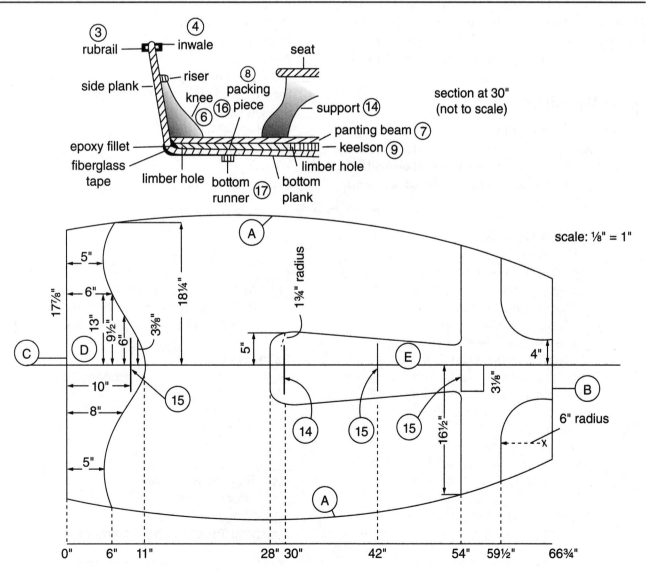

Building Uqbar

Step-by-Step Instructions with Illustrations

Use these step-by-step instructions when building any model in the Uqbar series. They were written specifically for Uqbar 8, so you can follow them exactly when building that boat. If you're building any of the other models, you'll note some differences in dimensions and also in some of the construction details. Therefore, if you're building one of the other model Uqbars, be sure to incorporate the variations noted in the appropriate chapter for the specific model you're building.

Tools Required

The following is a list of tools you'll need to build an Uqbar. The only electric tools necessary are an ordinary drill and a simple jigsaw with a plywood blade. If you have the use of additional electric tools such as a sander

or a circular saw for cutting straight lines, by all means use them!

___Tape measure, pencil, 3' ruler (yardstick)
___Framing square or equivalent right angle
___Simple jigsaw with plywood-cutting blade
___Electric drill
___Pliers, cutting pliers
___Screwdrivers
___Awl
___Block plane or scraper
___Sanding blocks (electric sander optional)
___Straight backsaw
___Chisel
___Mallet or hammer
___Wrench
___Clamps (or screws)

Steps at a Glance

___Preparing and Working with Epoxy
___Preparing the Plywood Parts
___Step 1. Trace and Cut Plywood Parts
___Step 2. Predrill Matching Holes
___Step 3. Cut Seat Risers
___Step 4. Chamfering the Hull Parts
___Step 5. Beveling the Seats
___Step 6. Coating Parts with Epoxy
___Assembling the Hull
___Gluing on the Seat Risers
___Gluing on the Keelson
___Filleting the Inside Seams
___Preparing for Installation of Doublers
___Fiberglassing the Outside Seams
___Gluing on the Transom Doublers
___Feathering the Fiberglass Tape
___Installing the Skeg and Bottom Runners

___Installing the Rubrails
___Installing the Oarlock Pads and Inwales
___Installing the Seats for U7, U8, U10
___Additional Steps for Outboard Use
___Reinforcing the Transom—Knees
___Pad for Outboard Motor Clamp
Sailboats Only
___King Plank and Daggerboard Trunk
___Lower Gudgeon Pad
___Tow-Eye
___Mast Step
___Daggerboard
___Kick-Up Rudder and Tiller
Installing the Hardware
___Oarlock Sockets (All Models)
___Sailing Hardware
Finishing Touches and Comments

Preparing and Working with Epoxy

The instructions in this book refer to the WEST SYSTEM epoxy. (See *http://www.westsystem.com.*) You may prefer to use another brand of epoxy, in which case you'll need to follow the manufacturer's instructions. Whatever epoxy you use, be sure that it's top grade; scrimping on the material that holds your boat together would be unwise.

No matter which brand of epoxy you use, it can be mixed with microballoons, fibers, and hardeners for various purposes. We'll use four mixes, the makeup of which depends on whether we intend to use the mix normally (i.e., the "Basic Mix"), as glue, as fillet material, or as a coating for the plywood.

Epoxy Mix Definitions

Basic Mix: 5 parts epoxy + 1 part fast hardener (Note: the WEST SYSTEM provides pumps that automatically dispense the proper ratio of epoxy to hardener.)

Gluing Epoxy: Basic Mix + microfibers (heavy syrup consistency)

Filleting Epoxy: Basic Mix + ½ microfibers and ½ microballoons, or prepackaged filleting blend (peanut butter consistency)

Coating Epoxy: Warm epoxy (without hardener) to about 80 degrees F. Then mix in slow hardener. Surfaces being coated must be at least 60 degrees F.

Epoxy has what's known as a working time or pot life: the length of time the material can be used before it begins to harden and thus becomes difficult to work with. Working times are dependent on the type of hardener used and on the temperature. In general, pot life is 20 minutes at 65 degrees F and 10 minutes at 75 degrees F. (These times could vary somewhat, especially if you're using something other than WEST SYSTEM epoxy.)

Be sure to mix only small quantities at a time. Otherwise the mixture will become hot and harden before you can use it. (Mixing together epoxy resin and hardener produces heat—in other words, it creates an *exothermic* reaction. That reaction is what helps cure the epoxy.)

Surface Preparation

Before applying epoxy for whatever purpose, all surfaces must be dry, clean, and free of grease (including body oils). When in doubt, wipe surfaces with acetone or alcohol. Roughen surfaces with coarse sandpaper for gluing.

Epoxy can be used very effectively to fill gaps. Fill in gaps with thick epoxy to create the strongest joint.

Epoxy hardeners are tough on skin, and contact with them can cause irritation or a rash. Therefore, avoid getting epoxy (especially pure hardener) on clothing. Soap, warm water, and a Dobie pad (the type usually used for scrubbing Teflon pans) will do a good job of cleaning your hands. Vinegar also works well. It is advisable, however, to use disposable gloves or barrier cream to minimize contact as much as possible.

Safety Note: concentrated epoxy fumes can cause irritation of the eyes, throat, and lungs, and repeated exposure has been known to cause asthma and other chronic respiratory problems. Thus, it's important to work in a well-ventilated space and to wear a face mask. (Cured epoxy is inert and therefore harmless, but sanding epoxy produces potentially harmful dust, so the same cautions apply when sanding.)

Preparing the Plywood Parts

Even if you've never built a birdhouse, let alone a boat, preparing the plywood for the Uqbar dinghy is fairly straightforward. You'll have to measure, draw some lines, mark some points, and eventually cut along the lines you drew. That's all there is to it.

Step 1. Trace and Cut Plywood Parts

(Refer to the cutting diagrams for the size dinghy you have chosen.)

Caution: remember the old adage "Measure thrice, cut once."

Bottom Plank

1. Draw a *centerline* 20" from and parallel to one long side of your plywood sheet.
2. Draw perpendiculars every 10", per the diagram.
3. Plot on these lines the points defining the chine, symmetrically on both sides of the centerline. Each of the points will be the distance from the centerline noted in the diagram for the size boat you've chosen. For example, on the U8 model diagram, you will set eight nails and will thus mark eight points; the middle point will be 20" out from the centerline. The two on either side of that middle point will be 19¾" and 19½", respectively, from the centerline. Continue plotting as noted in the appropriate diagram.
4. Tack nails at each of the points, and bend a batten around the nails, on the inside of each nail.
5. Trace around the batten.
6. Remove the nails.
7. Cut along the traced line.

Side Planks

1. Trace the baseline as per the diagram, with perpendiculars every 10".
2. On each of the perpendiculars, mark three series of points: for the *sheer*, the *seat riser*, and the chine.
3. As before, tack nails through those points, bend a batten, and trace.
4. Cut (sheer and chine only).
5. Cut the second side plank by tracing the one you just cut. Don't forget to draw the seat riser line.

Seat and Transoms

For the U7, draw symmetrically on your plywood stock since the cutting diagram provided shows only a half-breadth (half the seat), and then cut. On all the other models, the seats are very simply shaped; just draw and cut as indicated on the diagram. See the appropriate diagram for the correct dimensions.

Transom Doublers

A transom doubler is exactly what it sounds like: a piece of plywood glued to the outside of a transom to provide extra strength. These doublers should be ⅜" wider on either side than the transoms proper. (Keep in mind that Uqbar dinghies are essentially double-transomed: the forward transom—at the bow—is simply narrower than the aft transom.) Cut two ¼" pieces for each transom, and laminate for ½" thickness. (Alternatively, you could simply use a piece of ½" plywood.)

Step 2. Predrill Matching Holes, ⅛" in Diameter (30 minutes)

Drill these holes about every 6", ⅜" from the edge; see below.

1. Place the aft transom on the bottom plank so that the matching edges are superpimposed.
2. Drill through both pieces at the same time.
3. Do the same for the bow transom.
4. Superimpose the two side planks and drill holes alongside the bottom edge every 6" except toward the bow, where the holes should be drilled every 3". Do not try to drill matching holes in the bottom plank at this time.
5. Superimpose the transom so that one of its side edges is on the side plank's matching edge, and then drill.
6. Place the second edge in the same position, and drill exactly symmetrically.
7. In the bottom plank, drill only the two or three

first holes, corresponding to the ones in the side plank, starting from aft. You'll drill the others as you proceed to ensure that they'll match.

Step 3. Cut Seat Risers

1. Cut the aft seat riser from your 1½" × ¾" stock.
2. Cut the forward seat riser from your 4" × ¾" plank (4" wide because the tow-eye will go through it).
3. Bevel the aft and side risers (two *parting strips*) 15 degrees on top; the forward riser is beveled 55 degrees on top. See Figure 1.

Step 4. Chamfering the Hull Parts (20 minutes)

Tools needed: Block plane or surform scraper.

1. Identify and set aside the parts labeled BOTTOM, SIDE PLANKS (2), and AFT TRANSOM.
2. Lay the four parts down inside up on any flat surface, as illustrated in Figure 2.
3. Chamfer the inside bottom edges of these parts to help align them properly when wiring them together. The chamfer does not need to be terribly accurate, and should extend no more than ⅛".
4. In the same way, chamfer the *keelson* on both sides. (See Figure 3.)

Step 5. Beveling the Seats (15 minutes)

Tools needed: Block plane or surform scraper.

Bevel the sides of the seats to make them conform to the angles where they meet the topsides and transoms. The bevels are 15 degrees except for the forward edges of the forward seat, which is 55 degrees.

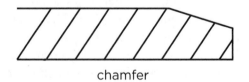

chamfer

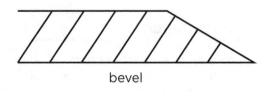

bevel

Figure 1. Note the somewhat subtle difference between a chamfer and a bevel. You will create both.

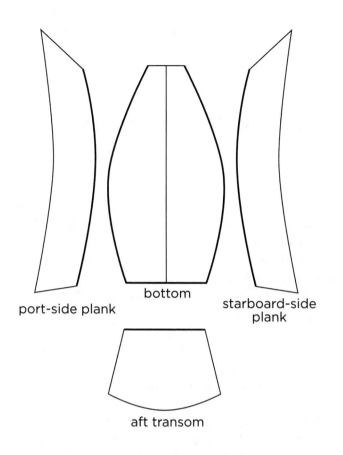

Figure 2. For exact dimensions of these and other parts, see the cutting diagram for your size boat.

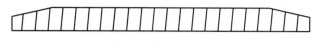

chamfering the
keelson

Figure 3. A chamfered keelson.

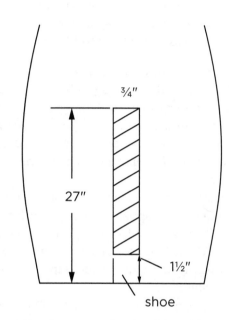

Figure 4. The dimensions for the skeg cutout.

Step 6. Coating Parts with Epoxy (1 hour)

(**Optional**) This step can be skipped, at least for the time being, particularly if you're working in a confined area or if your shop temperature is less than 65 degrees F. However, you should coat the inside of the boat at some point. Doing so adds strength and provides a barrier to water that might otherwise be splashed in and absorbed by the wood.

Preparation (15 minutes)

1. Take a sheet of plastic (or use garbage bags that have been cut open) and spread it on your work area.
2. Place the following parts on the plastic, making sure they don't touch one another:
   Hull panels (bottom, top sides, aft and bow transoms)—INSIDE up
   Keelson—TOP SIDE up (i.e., chamfered edge up)
   Seats (3)—UNDERSIDE up

Sailboat Models, also place:
   King plank and king plank doubler: UNDER-SIDE up
   Trunk cheeks: INSIDE up
   If your workspace is not big enough for all the parts, just coat a few parts at a time. Epoxy takes about 3 to 4 hours to dry at 70 degrees F, longer in lower temperatures. Below 40 degrees F, most epoxy simply will not dry or cure properly and may become difficult to work with or may require special handling, hardeners, etc. If you do the hull panels first, you can begin assembling them while the other parts are curing, but be sure that the hull parts have cured first.
3. Make sure all parts are clean, dry, and free of dust. It is a good idea to wipe them with a cloth impregnated with alcohol or acetone. (Do *not* use paint thinner, gas, or kerosene.) The wood should be at a temperature of 60 degrees F or more.
4. You'll use a small roller with sponge roller covers, and disposable brushes. They should also be at 60 degrees F or more.

Mix and Apply Epoxy (45 minutes)

WEST SYSTEM is a popular two-part epoxy that consists of an epoxy resin, multiple types of hardeners designed to work in varying temperatures, and pumps that automatically dispense the appropriate amount of each. You may choose to use a different brand of epoxy, of course. If so, be sure to follow the mixing and application instructions for the brand you've selected. Broadly speaking, the following instructions apply to most types of marine-grade epoxy systems, but they specifically assume that you're using WEST SYSTEM epoxy.

1. Prepare a very small quantity of epoxy at a time, until you get used to working with it. After you acquire more experience with the epoxy, you may opt to mix larger quantities. But do start with very little, since it is easy to make a mistake, resulting in your epoxy mix jelling in the pot and having to be discarded.

2. In separate containers, measure about ¼ cup epoxy resin and the appropriate amount of hardener, as specified by the manufacturer. (If you are using the WEST SYSTEM pumps, then one squirt of each will dispense the required 5-to-1 ratio. Do not mix at this point.)

3. Warm the epoxy resin to about 70 to 75 degrees F (without hardener). Caution: do not overheat.

4. Mix in the hardener thoroughly. You'll have about 10 minutes in which to work before the epoxy starts jelling in the pot and becomes unmanageable.

5. Pour the warm epoxy directly on the plywood; using the roller, roll the epoxy evenly and thinly on all parts. Press hard. Work fast, since pot life at this temperature is short, and the roller sleeve will quickly become gummy. You'll see that at this temperature, the epoxy is quite liquid and spreads easily. If you haven't mixed enough epoxy, don't worry and don't rush. After you have finished using the first batch, prepare another batch in the same way.

6. Check the chamfered edges to be sure they are well impregnated with epoxy. If necessary, go over them again with more epoxy and a disposable brush.

7. Remove the roller sleeve from the roller and discard. Wipe off all spills and drips and wash your hands.

8. Allow the epoxy to cure. You can apply a second coat after the first has cured, or you can wait until after the boat is built to do that. Note that the first coating tends to raise the grain. For smoothness, you may want to sand between coats, but don't sand the bottom: it will remain just rough enough to be non-skid.

Assembling the Hull (2 hours)

Tools needed: pliers, cutting pliers, drill (for extra holes as needed)

(See the Visual Guide, photos 1 to 9, pages 9–11.)

Before assembling, lightly trace centerlines on both sides of the transoms and bottom plank. On the underside of the bottom plank, also trace a line parallel to, and 10" on either side of, the centerline. (These are for the bottom runners.)

You are now ready to assemble the hull with the copper wire.

1. Cut the wire into 6" lengths. You'll need about six dozen pieces.

2. Lay bottom, sides, and transoms INSIDE up (i.e., chamfer up).

3. Start by wiring the AFT TRANSOM to the BOTTOM. Lay the aft transom flat on top of the bottom so that the predrilled holes correspond, chamfers inside.

   Thread copper wires through the matching holes, and twist the two outer ends loosely together by hand, so that after wiring the transom is free to swivel back to its almost vertical position. (See Figure 5.)

4. Starting on the starboard side, wire the sides to the bottom and to the aft transom.

   First, lay the side plank facedown on the bottom, so that a few of the aft holes correspond. Then wire.

   Then swivel the side to an almost vertical position, so that you can wire the uppermost holes of the side and transom together.

   Now the transom and side will hold together by themselves, although they'll be quite wobbly at this stage.

5. Place a few more wire-ties loosely on the seam side/bottom, proceeding forward; also finish wiring the side plank to the transom.

6. Install the port-side plank in the same way.

7. Tighten everything before proceeding.

   Support the free-hanging forward part of the side planks in order to bring the side/bottom firmly together at the very aft holes. Tighten.

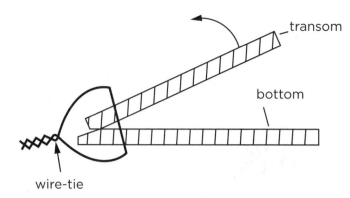

Figure 5. Note that the wire-ties holding the transom to the bottom are, at this point, loose enough to allow the transom to "flop" about.

Similarly, tighten the transom/bottom wires. Be careful to center the transom so that it is positioned correctly.

8. Note that there may remain a small gap toward the lower corner where all three planks join. It's OK to have a small gap, but try to make these gaps equal on the port and starboard sides.

Continue wiring the side/bottom, proceeding forward equally on port and starboard. Tighten firmly as you go, making sure the side/bottom seam is tolerably even all around. Consistency is the goal here rather than achieving a perfect seam. If the side rides mostly outside the bottom, that's fine as long as it's consistent all around. Or if the bottom is outside the sides, that's also OK as long as it's consistent all around.

9. Place the forward transom facedown on the bottom plank, and wire it at the foot, as you did for the aft transom. Don't wire it too tightly; it must be free to swivel upward.

10. Swivel the forward transom into position. You'll have to force the sides apart. Tie the transom to the sides through the holes second from the top to hold it in position. Then tighten the bottom wire-ties.

11. Now place and tighten all remaining wire-ties between the transom and the sides. Do not hesitate to apply some force here and there, even to the extent of using a large screwdriver as a lever; your goal is to align the bending transom exactly to the sides. Don't worry if the plywood splinters slightly.

12. If necessary, drill more holes and insert additional wire-ties to hold the sides firmly together and reduce all the gaps. You may place the wires practically on top of each other if necessary; they'll be covered with epoxy fillets eventually.

13. Go over the whole boat and check that all of the wire-ties are tight. Replace any that may have broken during tightening.

14. Note that the most difficult place to achieve a tight fit is at the forefoot. Don't worry if a small gap (up to ⅜") remains there. Try to even the gaps on both sides to preserve symmetry.

Then, before filleting, cover the gaps on the outside with duct or masking tape to help hold in the fillet. You'll apply a generous epoxy fillet on the inside and fair on the outside, and the result will be a neat seam that's as strong as possible.

Gluing on the Seat Risers (1 hour)

Tools/materials needed: screwdriver, temporary #6 × ⅝" screws with washers, awl, and 1 homemade clamp. (See the Visual Guide, pages 11–12, photos 10 to 12.)

1. Glue the seat risers to the side panels, with their tops even with the pretraced line. All seat risers are ¾" short at each end in order to leave space for filleting. Note: when gluing two pieces together, if one has been previously coated with epoxy, then spread the glue only on the other. If none has been coated, then spread the glue on both.

2. If you have enough clamps, just glue the risers

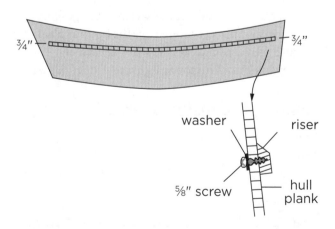

Figure 6. Use temporary screws to hold the seat risers in place. If you plan to leave the screws permanently in place, use flathead rustproof screws and countersink them.

in position. If, as is most likely, you do not have enough clamps, proceed as follows. (See Figure 6.)

Hold the risers against the side in their approximate position, using the homemade clamp or any other convenient device.

From outside, drive the temporary screws through the washers to hold the risers in position while the glue sets. The wood is soft, so it should not be necessary to drill; just punch a pilot hole with an awl. If you'd rather leave the screws in, use flathead rustproof screws and countersink them.

Begin amidships, proceed aft, then forward.

A double curvature occurs toward the bow; you may have to exert force and put in more screws than you used on the aft section in order to counteract the twist.

The aft and bow transom risers are straight: a couple of screws should be enough.

Gluing on the Keelson (30 minutes)

1. Before gluing on the keelson, you will have to give the bottom its proper rocker, or fore and aft curvature. A single spreader in the center will do the trick.

   Use the center seat for U7, U8, and U10 models.

   For U6, since there is no middle seat, just cut a batten ¾" × 1½" × 40" long, notched to accommodate the seat risers, and clamp or screw it 30" forward of the transom as measured directly from the top of the transom riser. This batten will later be discarded. If the seat buckles a little, stiffen it with a batten.

2. Coat the underside of the keelson with gluing epoxy and place, centered, on the bottom plank. Be sure the keelson clears the wires at each end. A few weights placed on top will ensure proper adhesion.

Filleting the Inside Seams (2 hours)

Tools/materials needed: squeegees, plywood paddles, disposable brushes, rags.

(See the Visual Guide, pages 12–13, photos 13 to 16.)

Preparation

1. Check once again that all the wire-ties are tight; there should be no wobbling.

2. Using a blunt instrument, such as a large screwdriver, push in each wire-tie against the

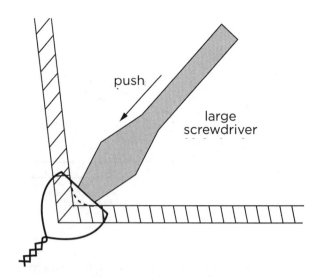

Figure 7. Use a large screwdriver to force the wire so that it lies more or less flat against the inside seam.

inside seam so that the wire tends to lie against the wood. (See Figure 7.)

Note: uneven tension on the wire-ties may result in a slight twist of the hull. To make sure the boat is even, place the assembly on a flat surface, and support the forefoot and stern with some blocks of the appropriate height for your model dinghy:

U6: forefoot 2½" high, transom 2" high

U7, U8, U10: forefoot 5½" high, transom 3" high

Make sure that the boat is sitting flat amidships. If either side is lifted, place weights inside where appropriate to bring it down. Remember that after filleting, that shape will be permanent.

3. Cut the corner of a squeegee to form an oval "paddle" to help shape the epoxy fillet. (Alternatively, you may make one out of plywood.) Also, prepare 1"-wide plywood sticks to spread the filleting epoxy into the seam.

4. Filleting mixture: Mix a small quantity of epoxy and hardener in the usual proportion of 5 to 1. Then stir in a mixture of thickeners composed of about half microballoons (or tan filleting mixture) and half microfibers. (Alternatively, use a prepackaged filleting blend.) The epoxy will absorb quite a bit of these thickeners. Continue adding until the well-mixed resin attains the consistency of peanut butter at room temperature: firm enough that it will not sag, malleable enough that it is easy to spread.

Remember that pot life is only about 20 minutes at 70 degrees F, and less at higher temperatures. Mix only the quantity you can handle in that time.

Filleting

It takes a bit of practice to achieve a clean fillet, so if you have never made one, you may wish to begin where it won't show. If so, start with the seams between the bottom and aft transom and the bottom and bow transom. (These will eventually be covered by the seats, so if they're not quite as neat as they should be, no one will be the wiser.)

Filleting requires spreading the filleting material into the seam, forming the fillet to the size and shape desired, and finally cleaning up the fillet. We'll take each step one by one.

1. Spread the filleting material into the seam.

    A flat stick works well for taking material from the mixing pot and applying it to the seams. Apply more material rather than less (you can always add more later). Make sure the seam is well filled in. Use the stick to push the excess farther along the seam. Spread the whole contents of your mixing pot this way. You should have mixed just about enough to cover at most 10" of the seam.

    Important: resist the temptation to make large fillets: the best fillet is the smallest one possible (just enough to entirely cover the copper wire) and as even as possible. A larger fillet would only create hard spots.

2. Form the fillet. (See Figure 8.)

    Hold your squeegee (or plywood paddle) at a right angle to the panels so the radiused angle

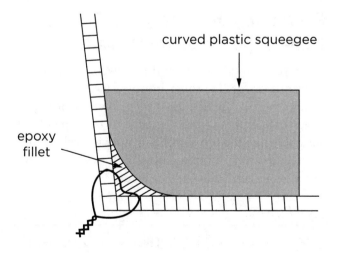

epoxy
fillet

curved plastic squeegee

Figure 8. Use a shaped squeegee or paddle for filleting. It takes practice to be able to create a neat fillet.

is in the seam. Form the fillet by making one pass to remove excess mixture. You can further control the depth and shape of the fillet by changing the angle at which you hold your paddle. With a little experience, you'll be able to make a neat fillet with a single pass.

Make the pass firmly so that any excess material is deposited farther along the seam. If your fillet doesn't look great, don't worry; you can always fill in hollows or sand off high spots later. The important thing is to fill the seam and cover the wire.

3. For extra strength at the forefoot, apply a strip of fiberglass.

    Cut a strip to fit, long enough to overlap the sides about 1".

    Push the strip into the fillet you applied at the bottom/forward transom seam. Do it immediately, while the fillet is wet.

    Coat the fiberglass tape with nonthickened epoxy (Basic Mix) to fill in the weave. Wipe off excess. Allow to cure.

    To improve looks and strength, follow the same procedure for the vertical seams between the bow and aft transoms and the side planks.

4. Clean up.

    Epoxy bonds to epoxy for 100% strength, even to already-cured epoxy. As you go along, or anytime you take a break, make sure that everything is cleaned up. Use a putty knife or sharpened stick to remove excess material before it hardens. Also wipe or scrape off all drippings.

    Keep in mind that removing cured epoxy takes a good deal of sanding, sweating, and cursing. You're bound to spill some; just remember to wipe it up before it hardens.

Preparing for Installation of Doublers

Next you'll be fiberglassing the outside seams of your boat and then gluing on the transom doublers that you created earlier. (See Figure 9 on page 67.)

Transom doublers are glued to the transom in order to strengthen it. It will simplify your work if, after fiberglassing the seams, you immediately install the transom doublers—before the epoxy on the seams has time to cure. This will eliminate the need for sanding.

Begin as follows:

1. Hold the doublers against the transoms, making sure the straight side is parallel to the bottom and the top slightly overlaps the top of the transom (¼"

at most) to facilitate later fairing. (The sides will also overlap slightly, to be trimmed after gluing.)

2. Trace each doubler onto the transom and make a few surmarks (reference marks) so that you'll be able to reposition them exactly at a later time.

3. If you're going to use screws to hold the doublers in position while the glue sets (see "Gluing on the Transom Doublers," step 2), then prepare pilot holes.

Fiberglassing the Outside Seams (1½ hours)

Materials needed: file, block plane, surform scraper, scissors, sandpaper, snipping pliers.

(See the Visual Guide, pages 13–15, photos 17 to 25.)

Preparation

1. After the inside fillets have cured, turn the boat over.

2. Snip off the copper wire as close to the wood as possible.

3. File protruding copper wires flush.

4. Fair all seams to a radius of about ¼". First, knock off the sharp edge with a block plane or scraper. Then, using coarse sandpaper, round the seams. (Gouges from the coarse sandpaper will help the fiberglass and epoxy to adhere, so don't worry about those.) See Figure 10.

5. Cut the fiberglass tape into segments of the proper length. Allow for overlapping. Set aside.

Execution

Now you'll fill in all wire holes and other voids and epoxy the tape in place, completing one seam at a time.

1. Prepare a very small quantity of epoxy putty, but make it quite a bit looser than your filleting mixture. This time add only the microballoons or tan filleting compound; no microfibers are needed.

2. With a putty knife, fill in all the holes or cracks generously, one seam at a time.

3. Prepare a small batch of Basic Epoxy Mix (resin plus hardener). Note: the ratio can be different with different epoxies. Brush it on the seam, at the same time spreading the excess epoxy before it hardens.

4. Unroll the tape onto the wet seams, and smooth with your fingers. (Use disposable gloves to protect your hands.)

5. Brush more epoxy on top of the tape to fill in the weave. (For the layer of epoxy on top of the tape, a pinch of colloidal silica added to the basic mix will help thicken the mixture.)

A saturated tape is translucent. If white spots appear, add more epoxy. (You may have to lift the tape to put epoxy beneath it. Then push the tape back on, making sure good contact is established with the wood.)

6. Proceed in the same way for the next seam, overlapping tape at the corners.

Proceed immediately to the next step without waiting for the epoxy to cure.

Gluing on the Transom Doublers (20 minutes)

(See Figure 9.)

Materials needed: clamps, or screws with screwdriver and awl.

(See the Visual Guide, pages 15–16, photos 26 to 28.)

1. Prepare gluing epoxy, coat the matching surfaces on the doublers and the transom, and install as previously marked.

2. Hold with clamps; make sure the two pieces are in contact. If you don't have enough clamps, use temporary screws: either 1" screws driven from inside (with a protective pad) into the doublers wherever needed, or 1½" screws driven from the outside into a ¾"-thick temporary pad placed on the inside. In the latter case, you will need to make pilot holes.

Feathering the Fiberglass Tape (time depends on tools used)

Note: you can do this operation now, or later at your convenience; see "Finishing Touches," page 75.

Feathering the fiberglass tape means sanding the edges in such a way that the edge of the tape blends smoothly into the plywood. Sandpaper is used for these tasks, either with "potato power," as they say in Maine, or with an electric sander. (See Figure 11.)

By Hand

Using "potato power," this will take roughly 3 hours. Use a sheet of rough sandpaper wrapped around a wooden block approximately 6" × 2" × 2".

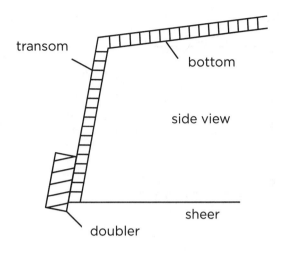

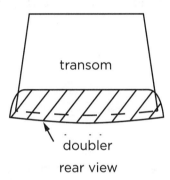

Figure 9. Gluing the doubler. Note that the top of the doubler extends beyond the top of the transom. You'll fair this later.

Using Electric Power

You can speed up the job by using an electric drill, belt sander, or a rotary sander of semi-professional or professional quality.

Electric drill (2 hours). Use a disc sanding attachment. Mount the roughest sanding discs available, or cut discs out of rough sandpaper. When sanding, hold the center of the disc over the fiberglass tape, allowing the edge to extend just slightly over the plywood.

Belt sander or professional sander (1 hour). These are high-powered machines and they remove material (fiberglass, wood, fingers) very quickly. Be sure you know what you are doing. It's very easy to make a mistake and sand off the fiberglass tape entirely or to gouge the plywood. Use medium sandpaper belts or discs to minimize possible damage.

Safety note: beware of the fiberglass dust; wear a dust mask.

If you completely sand off the fiberglass tape here and there, just cut a piece of tape large enough to cover the area (one piece per area), mix an adequate quantity of Basic Epoxy Mix, apply the tape, and spread more epoxy on top.

If you have made gouges in the bare plywood, you can ignore them for now. You will eventually fill them with epoxy putty. If the gouges go through the tapes, fill the gouge with epoxy putty, and without waiting for the putty to cure, apply the fiberglass tape as described above.

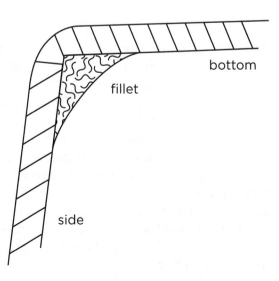

Figure 10. After you turn the boat over, you'll trim the wire, file any protruding ends flush, and sand the seams.

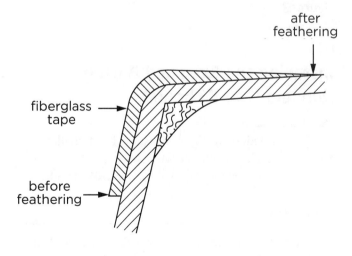

Figure 11. Feathering the fiberglass tape. Note the difference between the feathered (top right) and unfeathered (lower left) portions.

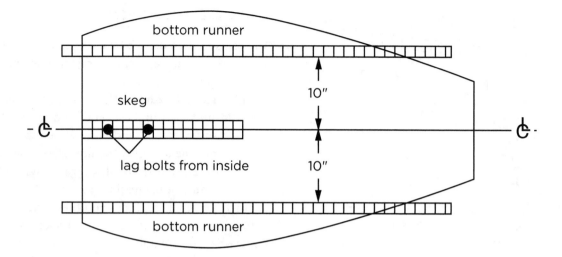

Figure 12. Note the position of the skeg (centered) and the bottom runners, each of which is (on U8, at any rate) placed 10″ out from the centerline.

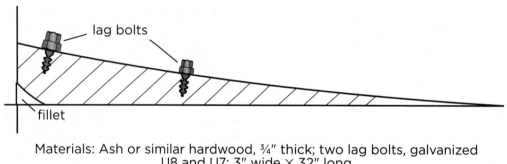

Materials: Ash or similar hardwood, ¾″ thick; two lag bolts, galvanized
U8 and U7: 3″ wide × 32″ long
U10: 5″ wide × 48″ long
U6: 3″ wide × 24″ long

Figure 13.

Installing the Skeg and Bottom Runners (1 to 1½ hours)

(See Figure 12.)

Tools needed: straight backsaw, chisel, mallet (or hammer), drill, screwdriver, wrench.

(See the Visual Guide, page 16, photos 29 to 30.)

The Skeg

Center the skeg on the bottom, outside, flush with the transom, and trace. Make sure the skeg fits snugly, and don't worry about irregularities; they will be evened out with epoxy. Then proceed as follows:

1. Remove the skeg, and make two pilot holes through the keelson to mark the placement of the *lag bolts*. The first pilot hole should be about 2″ forward of the transom, and the other is 10″ forward of the transom, centered.

2. If necessary, shave the skeg so that it conforms to the curvature of the hull.

3. Prepare thick gluing epoxy and spread it generously to take care of any irregularities. Push in the skeg until epoxy oozes out. If it doesn't ooze out, add more until it *does*. Add enough microballoons to the remaining mix to make filleting epoxy, and fillet on both sides of the skeg (a ¼″ radius is sufficient). Hold the skeg in place with weights until it is cured.

4. After it has cured, remove the temporary screws; turn the boat over and enlarge the pilot holes for the lag bolts through the center of the keelson

(³⁄₁₆" pilots for the thread; ¼" pilots for the shank). Tighten through oversize washers to spread the load. (See Figure 13.)

Note: it's easier to install the lag bolts before the epoxy cures, if you happen to have a helper who can hold the skeg while you push in the bolts from inside the boat. You will apply the fillets after tightening the bolts.

Bottom Runners

The bottom runners are glued parallel to the centerline, 10" on either side. Use weights or ¾" temporary screws to hold them in place until the glue cures. Then remove.

Installing the Rubrails (1 hour)

(See Figure 14.)

Tools/materials needed: screwdriver, small clamps and/or screws (either #6, ⅝" or non-rust #8 × ⅝", flathead).

A rubrail is meant to protect the hull and gunwale of your boat from wear imparted by the lines used to dock or guide the boat as well as from minor collisions with a dock or with other boats. They can be made of rubber, brass, or other materials; in this case, of course, the rubrail is made of wood.

1. Trim the doublers. Use a small-toothed handsaw against the topsides and in the same plane to ensure a continuous line for the rails. Watch the bevels—make sure the trimmed doublers extend on the same plane as the hull.
2. Starting from aft, glue on the rubrails, flush with the sheer, overlapping the transom doublers. Coat matching surfaces with epoxy.
3. If you have enough clamps, even for one at a time, just install, making sure the rail is flush with the sheer. It is all right if the plywood protrudes here and there; you will plane it flush later.

   If you have only a few clamps: hold the rail

in position, one part at a time, starting aft. Drive in temporary screws from inside (#6, ⅝" long), as many as needed to ensure good contact. Remove after cure.

You may prefer to use permanent screws driven from inside (#8 × ⅝", flathead). Because you're using hardwood, you'll need to drill pilot holes in order to place the screws.

At this point the hull is permanently assembled and all outside parts are in place. Still needed are seats, partial inwales, and oarlock pads. In addition, sailing models will require the king plank and doubler, daggerboard trunk, mast step, and lower *gudgeon pad*.

Installing the Oarlock Pads and Inwales (1 hour)

(See Figure 15.)

Preparation

1. There are two rowing positions: one from the center seat and one from the forward seat. If you intend to use your boat mostly under sail, a single pair of oarlock sockets for the center seat position will suffice.
2. Oarlock pads are installed inside so that the tops are flush with the sheer.
3. Measure 8" to 9" aft of the center seat's aft edge, on the sheer. Do the same aft of the forward seat's aft edge. The pads are centered on those marks. (The four pads are cut from ½" plywood and measure about 5" × 3".)
4. Place the aft pad in position; mark and hold with a clamp.
5. Place the forward pad in position; trace and mark. Remove.
6. Butt the inwale against the aft pad, and clamp flush to the sheer. Mark where it will butt against the forward pad, and trim. Remove inwale and pad.

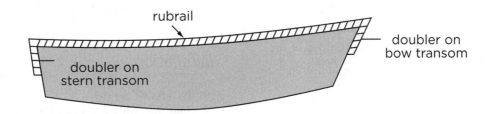

Figure 14. Rubrails run on port and starboard, with doublers at bow and stern transoms.

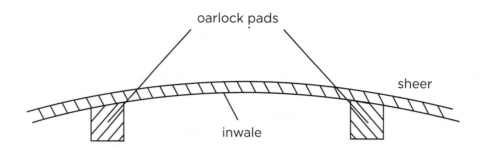

Figure 15. Oarlock pads mounted on inwales. The pads should be flush with the vessel's sheer..

Installation

The gluing sequence is aft pad, inwale, then forward pad. As usual, the glue will hold sufficiently, but for improved looks, you may want to drive permanent brass screws through the inwale (#8 × 1"). As this is hardwood, you will have to make countersunk pilot holes.

Installing the Seats for U7, U8, U10 (1½ hours)

(Note: U6 does not have a center seat.)

   Tools needed: block plane, scraper, screwdriver.
   (See the Visual Guide, photos 32 to 33.)
   The seats in the Uqbar dinghy are structural—that is, they are glued onto the seat risers and are reinforced by seat supports of ¾" × 1½" #2 pine installed athwartships, or across the boat. Those supports are beveled and notched at each end to conform to the curvature of the side plank and to fit around the risers.
   Note: if yours is a sailing model, the center seat forward support and the forward seat aft support are notched ¼" deep to receive the king plank. See below.

Preparation

1. The middle seat is cut to exact shape, but the aft and forward seats are cut slightly oversize to accommodate minor variations resulting from the building process.
2. The center seat is installed first. Its aft edge is placed as measured exactly from the top of the transom seat riser:
   U7: 35"
   U8: 36¾"
   U10: 44"
   (See plans for more specific examples.)

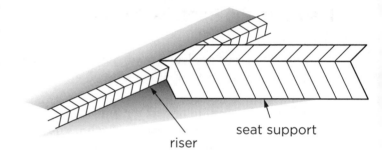

Figure 16. The seat supports are notched to fit correctly around the risers.

3. Position the center seat exactly on the risers, and hold in place with small clamps or by driving a couple of temporary screws into each riser.
4. Put seat supports in place. (See Figure 16.) You may have to file them slightly for an exact fit. To hold them in position, use small clamps or drive a temporary screw on each side close to the risers through the seat into the support.
5. You will now install the other seats in the same way. You may have to plane down the sides for a tight fit. In that case, plane both sides, alternately, and keep the bevel even.
6. Install the forward and aft seat supports as in Step 4 above.

Installation

1. Remove all parts.
2. Coat matching surfaces with gluing epoxy, applying a generous amount on the risers, and

clamp or screw back on, ensuring good contact throughout.

   Caution: if yours is a sailing model, be careful not to leave any drips in the cutouts for the king plank. Alternatively, you may wish to delay the gluing of the center and aft seats until you are ready to glue on the king plank and its doubler.

3. A blob of filleting epoxy pushed under the seats in the angle formed by the junction of the seat support and the side helps to consolidate everything.

Additional Steps for Outboard Use

Reinforcing the Transom—Knees

Using an outboard motor will put additional stress on the junction of the aft transom and side planks. The traditional way to reinforce this junction is to install knees. The hard-to-find traditional knee is made from a twisted root or branch that grew at almost a right angle.

   Here are three alternate ways to achieve the same result.

   Quick and dirty: use a ⅜" threaded brass rod and epoxy. (See Figure 17.) You won't actually be threading anything onto the rod, but the threads will provide a gripping surface for the epoxy.

   On each side:

1. Measure about 3" from the inside angle transom-side on both sides. Drill a ⅛" pilot hole at a 45-degree angle horizontally through the rubrail on one side and the transom on the other.
2. Enlarge the hole so that it will accommodate the threaded rod loosely. This is to leave room for thickened epoxy.
3. Coat the rod with thickened epoxy, and push epoxy into the holes.
4. Push in the rod so that it protrudes a little on each side. Allow to cure.
5. With a hacksaw, cut the rod flush, and coat the ends with epoxy.

   Simplified knee: use ash or a similar hardwood, permanent screws, and epoxy. (See Figure 18.) If you can find an appropriately crooked tree branch or root, use it! If not:

1. Use a piece of ash 2" thick × 2½" × 7".
2. Place it across the junction at a 45-degree angle. Trace. Cut.
3. Place it inside, under the inwale and flush with the transom. You will have to bevel the ends to conform closely to the two sides.
4. Dry-install with #8 permanent screws driven from outside the transom in, from outside the side plank

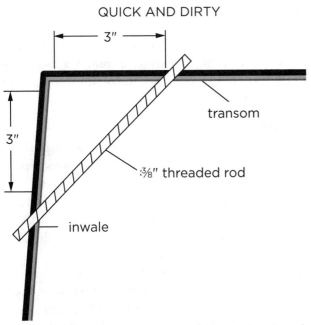

Figure 17. A "quick and dirty" knee made with a threaded rod.

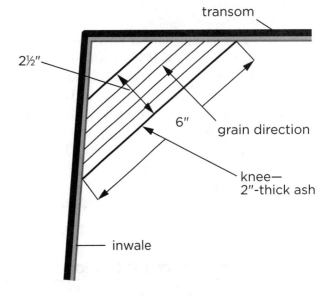

Figure 18. This simplified knee utilizes hardwood attached with permanent screws of two different sizes.

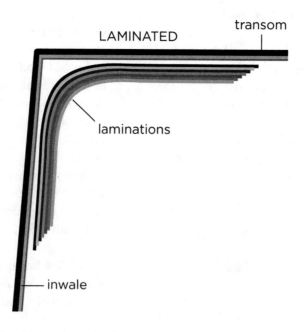

Figure 19. A laminated knee made with hardwood strips.

in, and #6 screws from the top of the inwale down. Use pilot holes.

Laminated knee: use ash or other similar hardwood, epoxy, and permanent screws. (See Figure 19.) With this method, we'll use the transom-to-side junction as a gluing jig. (Note that laminated knees are quite strong, sometimes even stronger than "grown" knees.)

1. Prepare flexible strips of ⅛" thick × 1" (or 1½") × 12". You'll need at least 6 strips on each side.
2. Protect the space on the boat with clear plastic held with duct tape or similar.
3. Dry-clamp the superimposed strips in the angle to make sure they'll take the curve without splitting.
4. Remove. Coat the strips with thickened epoxy.
5. Clamp them in position. Clean up and let cure.
6. Remove the knees, shape them with a jigsaw, and clean with a sander.
7. Insert epoxy and #8 rust-proof screws driven from outside the transom in, and from inside the knee out into the rubrail.
8. If any gap remains between knee and sides, fill with epoxy.

Pad for Outboard Motor Clamp

Place a piece of soft- or hardwood about ¾" thick × 5" × 6" on the inside of the transom, glued or screwed to the transom. For rowing/motoring models, place the pad centered. For sailboat models, place it offset to starboard, so that you can use the rudder.

If you're building a rowing or motoring model dinghy, construction is finished. Go to "Installing the Hardware," page 75.

Sailboats Only
King Plank and Daggerboard Trunk (1½ hours)

Note: if desired, instead of the built-in king plank-daggerboard/trunk-daggerboard combo, a single clip-on leeboard can be used. See instructions for U7, leeboard, page 32.

Preparation

1. Assemble the daggerboard trunk. If you haven't done so before, coat the inside of the cheek pieces with warm coating epoxy. As soon as you are sure there will be no drips, assemble the trunk as shown. (See the plans for your specific model.) The slot between the cheek pieces is ⅝" wide. Use gluing epoxy to assemble the trunk.
2. Cut and install the king plank and its doubler. The king plank is placed with its two ends in the notches provided in the center and forward seat supports, and the doubler is laminated to it, snugly fitted between the seats to form one continuous

surface. Just insert and glue. Let cure. (See Figure 20.)

3. In the king plank, cut out the slot for the assembled trunk. The outline of the slot is drawn on the king plank doubler. If the outline was erased during construction, note that the slot begins 6½" forward of the center seat's forward edge. To trace the shape, wait until the trunk assembly is dry, place it astride the centerline, and trace it; then cut.

4. Push the trunk assembly through the king plank slot so that the lower edge sits on the keelson, evenly and exactly centered. (See the plans for your specific model.) Trace the outline of the trunk onto the keelson, remove the trunk, and cut out the slot.

5. Slide the trunk back in through the king plank slot; then slide it through the bottom slot so that it is just about flush with the top of the king plank and the underside of the boat. The trunk has been cut slightly oversize. Let it protrude slightly both on top and bottom for gluing. You will trim it completely flush after the epoxy has cured.

Installation

1. Coat all matching surfaces with coating epoxy to ensure penetration. Then thicken your epoxy considerably, put some more epoxy on the inside of the slots, and push the trunk in.

2. If you have done your job well, the trunk will remain in position all by itself. If it is a bit loose, don't worry about it; just hold it in position with some nails toed in (i.e., driven in at an angle) at appropriate places.

3. Make some filleting epoxy. Push some of it inside any gap between the trunk and inside the cutouts; make a fillet around the trunk between the trunk and the bottom.

4. Make a fillet between the trunk and the underside of the king plank. This position is not easy to reach; however, it won't be seen, so just make sure that the fillet is as smooth as you can manage.

5. Carefully wipe off all surplus epoxy, particularly if there is any inside the trunk, where hardened drips would interfere with the daggerboard's up-and-down movements. Allow to cure.

6. After cure, trim and sand the top and bottom of the trunk flush with the top of the king plank and the bottom of the boat.

Lower Gudgeon Pad (15 minutes)

The function of this pad is to bring the lower gudgeon to the same plane as the upper one. Just glue in position as shown in Figure 21, holding in position with tape or temporary screws.

Tow-Eye

The tow-eye (a ⅜" × 2½" galvanized shoulder eye-bolt) is inserted through the forward seat riser, centered, just under the seat. Use an additional extra-large washer. (Here's a neat trick: to remove a metal fastener bedded in epoxy, heat the fastener with a soldering iron.)

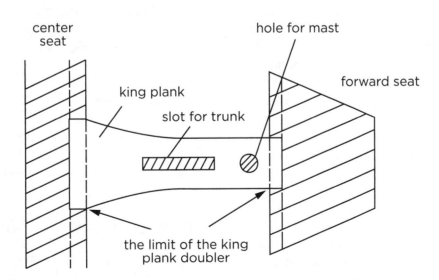

Figure 20. Bird's-eye view of the forward and center seats, plus king plank, on a U8.

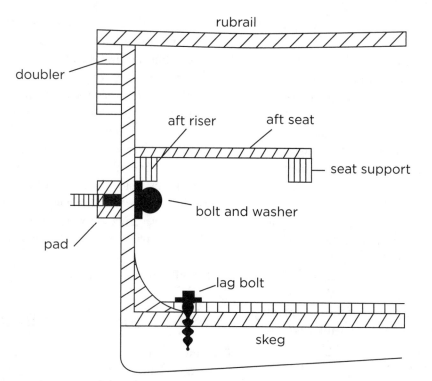

rubrail

doubler

aft riser   aft seat

seat support

bolt and washer

pad

lag bolt

skeg

Figure 21. Cross-section view of the aft seat supports, doublers, and lag bolts and washers. The lower gudgeon pad–which holds an eye that accepts a rudder pintle, allowing the rudder to swing freely (shown here)–is located beneath the aft seat.

Mast Step (15 minutes)

(See the plans for your specific model.)

1. Chock the boat so that it rests firmly on the skeg on a level surface.
2. Drill the vertical hole for the mast into the king plank/forward seat combo, as indicated on the plans for the appropriate model for your boat.
3. Slide the mast through the hole and center it vertically on the keelson. Use a level or plumb line to ensure that the mast is truly vertical. Where the mast meets the keelson is where you'll place the mast step.
4. Place the mast step wood block in position. Drill a hole in the block at the proper angle and the proper size for the diameter of the mast you're planning to use.
5. Slide the foot of the mast inside the hole in the mast step.
6. Check again to see that the mast is vertical and centered. Mark the place for the mast step.
7. Remove the mast, and glue the mast step on its mark. Use tape or temporary screws to hold it in place until cured.

Daggerboard (1 hour)

(See the plans for your specific model.)

1. Assemble the daggerboard by gluing the stop to the top edge of the daggerboard blade.
2. To reinforce the bond, drive three or four permanent screws (#8 × 1½") through the stop into the blade. (To do this, drill slightly oversize holes into the end grain, fill with epoxy, and push in the screws. This way, nothing will split.)
3. For a handle, drill two ³⁄₁₆" holes about 1½" deep, through the stop into the blade. Cut a piece of ¼" nylon or Dacron rope about 15" long. Fill the two holes with epoxy, and push the ends of the rope into the holes. Let cure.
4. The plug is assembled following the same steps as above.

Kick-Up Rudder and Tiller (1 hour)

1. The kick-up rudder consists of two flanges, a packing piece, and the blade. Laminate the two flanges with the packing piece. When cured, insert the blade into the space between the flanges. Drill

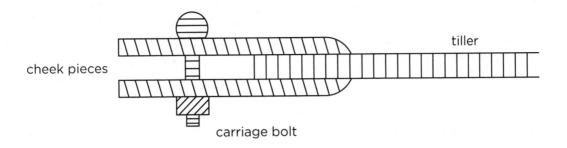

cheek pieces

tiller

carriage bolt

Figure 22. The tiller assembly consists of the tiller itself and two cheek pieces, held together with a carriage bolt.

the hole for the pivot (use a ⅜" bronze carriage bolt) through the flanges and blade. If yours is a plywood blade, a shock cord attached to the leading edge and led up to the tiller will serve to hold the blade down in the water.

2. The tiller comes in three pieces: the tiller itself and two cheek pieces. The tiller's thickness should be the same as the rudderhead. Assemble as shown in Figure 22. Glue is normally enough, but you may also use a couple of bronze screws on each side while the glue cures. If you prefer, you can then leave the screws in place. After curing, insert the rudderhead between the cheek pieces, and drill for a ⅜" bronze or stainless steel pivot.

Installing the Hardware

Install and then remove the hardware before the final sanding/finishing. That way if you make any errors, gouges, or marks during installation, they will be easy to correct.

Oarlock Sockets (All Models)

1. Use side-mounted oarlock sockets. Mount two pairs so you can change position for rowing according to load. The oarlocks proper should be the round type that remain permanently attached to the oars. Many prefer the look of the bronze oarlocks and sockets if the boat is to be *bright*—i.e., varnished but unpainted.

2. If you intend to use mainly an outboard motor or a sail, a single pair of sockets may suffice. In that case, the flop-down Davis type could be used, with the oarlock proper remaining attached to the socket, in one unit.

3. Using the proper screw size, as indicated by the manufacturer, screw in the sockets.

Sailing Hardware

Rudder fittings: Both gudgeons are fastened with bolts driven from outside. The bolts for the lower one can be a little too long, but the top one should be the exact size, so as not to protrude too much through the finishing washers on the inside, where they are visible. Install the corresponding lower pintle on the rudderhead, then place this pintle inside its gudgeon to determine the position of the upper pintle and gudgeon, generally about 2" below the sheer.

Sprit: Cut off the head of the brass or bronze #12 screw. Drill an oversize hole in the end grain; then fill with gluing epoxy and push in the screw. Allow to cure.

Cleats: The *downhaul* cleat is installed as low as possible on the aft face of the mast. (Leave about 1" of clearance above the *mast partner*—i.e., the point where the mast goes through the hole.) The snotter cleat is on one side, 6" to 8" above the boom. Note: unless you are an experienced sailor, do not install a cleat for the *sheet*. Instead, to minimize the possibility of capsizing, hold the sheet in your hand, ready to respond instantly to any shift in the wind.

Reeving holes: At this time, drill the holes for the lacing line (top of mast), for the snotter (bottom of sprit), for the blocks (both extremities of the boom), and in the transom about 4" on either side of the tiller for the rope traveler. Refer to the appropriate sail plan for exact location.

Finishing Touches and Comments

1. Remove all hardware except the tow-eye.
2. Cut rubrails flush with the outside of the transom doubler.
3. Cut the bottom runners flush with the bottom of the boat.
4. Feather the fiberglass tape if you have not already done so.

5. Round all edges with plane, surform tools, and sandpaper.
6. Go carefully over the whole boat inside and outside. Prepare a thick epoxy putty and fill in any gouges, holes, and gaps. Let cure.
7. Give the boat a general overall sanding so that all surfaces are clean and smooth.
8. Coat all bare surfaces with warm coating epoxy. Be sure not to miss anything. Let cure.
9. Replace the hardware.

Your boat is now protected. You can use your Uqbar dinghy with its epoxy coating only, but eventually it will deteriorate under the sun's ultraviolet rays. Fairly soon (perhaps before the next season) you should protect it with an ultraviolet filter, such as varnish or paint. Most people like their Uqbar dinghies finished bright. Some opt to paint the outside, the inside, or both. One inventive soul even inserted Plexiglas panels between the middle and aft seats to better contemplate the underwater scenery in the Bahamas!

Note that oars are an important and often overlooked item. They can cost as little as $20 a pair or as much as $250. Because Uqbar is very light, overly long oars do not work well. The best sizes are 5' oars for the U6 and U7 models and 6' oars for the U8 and U10 models.

Even if you plan to use your Uqbar mainly under sail or with a small outboard, keep a pair of oars on board. (Collapsible oars make for easy storage.) Never go sailing or motoring without oars aboard.

And remember, the U.S. Coast Guard requires one life jacket or PFD (personal flotation device) per person on any open boat. Do observe that sensible precaution.

Amidships. Roughly in the center of a boat, about halfway between bow and stern.

Batten. A long, thin, flexible piece of wood used to reinforce something, such as a wooden structure. Often refers to a piece of wood (or plastic) inserted in the leech of a sail, but here mostly used in the former sense. Also used to trace curves.

Bending Moment. The force required to bend a structure such that it meets another structure at the desired angle.

Bent. Tied or knotted to.

Bevel. A cut of any angle other than a 90-degree angle that extends the entire thickness of a plank, board, sheet, or other material.

Block. A pulley. Also a case with one or more sheaves or pulleys used to gain a mechanical advantage for raising a sail or other weight.

Bottom Runner. Thin fore-and-aft batten fastened to the bottom of a boat for protection.

Bow Transom. On a double-transomed boat, the flat outboard section of a boat at the bow, extending from keel to the topmost edge of the vessel's side.

Bright. Finished with varnish or oil so that the wood grain is visible. Such wood is often referred to as "brightwork."

Centerline. A line that bisects a plane. On a boat, a line measured from bow to stern along the center of the bottom of the hull, dividing the hull into two left and right sections.

Chamfer. Similar to a bevel, except that a chamfer does not extend the entire thickness of the plank, board, sheet, or other material.

Chine. The edge formed on the hull of a flat-bottomed boat at the point where the bottom joins the topsides.

Clew. The lower aft corner of a fore-and-aft sail.

Colloidal Silica. Silica particles used as a thickener for epoxy.

Daggerboard. A removable centerboard on a small sailboat that can be lowered into the water to serve as a keel. It is stowed in and lowered through a structure known as a daggerboard trunk.

Dinghy. A small boat used for recreation or as a tender for a larger vessel.

Dink. A slang term for a dinghy or tender.

Doubler. A piece of wood attached to planking to "double" its thickness as a way of adding strength.

Downhaul. A line with which a sail is tightened by pulling down, or is brought down entirely.

Dry-Clamp (or **Dry-Fit**). To fit or clamp without using any adhesive or fasteners, so as to check the fit of a part prior to attaching it permanently.

Epoxy. A strong, waterproof adhesive plastic or paint made from thermosetting polymers. Epoxy generally consists of two parts—resins and hardeners.

Exothermic. Heat-producing. For example, the heat that results when an epoxy resin and a hardener are combined.

Fair. As a verb: to smooth. As an adjective: without bulge or dimple.

Feather(ing). To reduce the thickness of an edge, in this context, to facilitate fairing. Often used as synonymous with fairing.

Fiberglass. A material made of glass fibers sealed in resins.

Fillet(ing). Pronounced "FILL-it," this is a smooth, neat bead (of epoxy, in this case) used to cover the inside corner where two pieces of plywood meet. A (usually wooden) filleting tool is used to apply the epoxy fillet.

Forefoot. The area on the hull of a boat at which the keel and stem or bow transom join.

Freeboard. The vertical distance between the water and the gunwale of a boat. The space between the deck and the level of the water.

Gudgeon Pad. A socket for a rudder pintle. A gudgeon pad can be used to help align gudgeons.

Gunwale. Pronounced "GUN-nel," the upper edge of the side of a boat.

Half-Breadth. A plan of one half of the hull of a vessel divided lengthwise amidships, showing water lines, stations, diagonals, and bow lines.

Inwale. A strip of wood attached inside the frame of a boat and used to reinforce the gunwale.

Jig. A device or frame used to hold work and to guide tools being used on the work.

Keelson. A longitudinal structure running above and fastened to the keel of a ship in order to stiffen and strengthen its framework. In Uqbar it consists of a simple 4"-wide piece of plywood.

Kick-Up Rudder. A rudder hinged such that it "kicks up" (rises) on a small sailboat that is beached. Also handy if the boat should run aground. (The alternative could be a broken rudder.)

King Plank. The center plank of a deck.

Knee. A curved piece of wood often used as a form of bracing in a boat or ship.

Lag Bolt. A heavy wood screw with a square or hexagonal head, normally driven in with a wrench rather than a screwdriver.

Leach (or **Leech**). The trailing edge of a sail.

Leeboard. A board attached to the side of a boat that's lowered into the water to reduce drift to the leeward side.

Limber Hole. A hole or channel that allows water to drain to the lowest point in a boat's hull.

Loose Footed. A sail that's attached to the boom only at the tack and clew.

Luan Plywood. A less expensive alternative to true marine-grade plywood, Luan features a solid core material sandwiched between two layers of veneer.

Luff. Here, the forward edge of a sail.

Mast Partner. A cutout in the forward section of the boat allowing the mast to be inserted.

Mast Step. A reinforced mounting platform on which the base (heel) of the mast is seated.

Oarlock. A rotating metal guide in a sleeve at the gunwale used to hold oars being pulled to propel a rowboat.

Panting Beam. A beam or section fitted athwartships in the bow or stern of a boat in order to prevent the hull from panting, or flexing in and out.

Parting Strip. A thin strip of wood or metal used to separate two adjoining materials.

Pintle. A pivoting hinge or bolt. On a boat, a vertical pin used to hold a rudder.

Pot Life. The length of time an epoxy-resin mix can be used before it begins to harden.

Pram. A flat-bottomed boat, usually with a squared-off (or nearly so) bow.

Reeve. To pass a rope through something, such as a block or a ring or bracket on a traveler.

Resin. A thick liquid that hardens into a semi-transparent solid. (Originally derived from plant secretions but now usually synthetic.)

Rocker. In this context, the fore and aft curve of a vessel's bottom or keel upward toward the transom and bow.

Rubrail. A board attached along the gunwale to reinforce the sheer; used to protect from damage at the dock.

Seat Riser. Seat support running from one side of a boat to the other.

Sheer. The fore-and-aft curvature from bow to stern of a boat's deck. The top edge of the side plank.

Sheet. On a boat, a sheet is not a sail but a line used to control the sails.

Skeg. The projecting stern section of a vessel's keel used to support the rudder. A small fin fitted aft of the keel to protect the rudder and propeller and improve steering and tracking.

Snotter Assembly. The rope figure-8 that holds the heel of a sprit to the mast on a sprit-rigged vessel.

Sprit. A light spar that crosses a sail diagonally.

Stitch-and-Glue. A boatbuilding technique in which plywood parts are "stitched" to one another with wire- (or occasionally nylon) ties.

Strongback. Temporary scaffolding used to hold parts together while working.

Tack. The lower forward corner of a fore-and-aft sail.

Toed In. Driven in at an angle.

Topsides. The visible outside of the hull. The outside face of the hull between the water and the deck—that is, the portion above the waterline.

Transom. The flat outboard section of a boat at the stern, extending from keel to the topmost edge of the vessel's side.

Traveler. On a larger vessel, a bracket mounted under the boom on a cabintop or deck to which the sheet block is secured, allowing the boom to move from side to side. On Uqbar, the traveler is a short length of rope mounted at the aft transom.

Trimaran. A fast sailboat with three parallel hulls. Trimarans are very stable and unlikely to capsize. However, when they do capsize, they're difficult to right.

WEST. A popular proprietary system of epoxies and resins.

Appendix B
Sources of Materials

Boatbuilding Lumber, Plywood, and Related Products

Normally the easiest source is your local lumberyard, since Uqbar does not use fancy plywood or lumber. In case you need to go farther afield, we provide below a list of suppliers. Many also advertise in publications such as *WoodenBoat, Professional BoatBuilder, National Fisherman, Good Old Boat, Small Craft Advisor,* and *Messing About in Boats.* WoodenBoat's *Boatbuilding Woods: A Directory of Suppliers* remains a useful though somewhat outdated (1993) source. This appendix also contains sources for other wood-related items.

Allied Veneer Company, 14711 Artesia Boulevard, La Mirada, CA 90638. Marine plywood including Joubert Okoume, Hydrotek, and Aquatek marine. *http://alliedveneer.com/*

Almquist Lumber Company, 5301 Boyd Road, Arcata, CA 95521. Boat woods and marine plywoods, including white oak, Douglas fir, Port Orford cedar, ipe, African mahogany, purpleheart, and teak. *http://www.almquistlumber.com/boatwoods.html/*

APA—The Engineered Wood Association, 7011 S. 19th Street, Tacoma, WA 98466-5333. *http://www.apawood.org/*

Boulter Plywood Corporation, 24 Broadway, Somerville, MA 02145. Teak, ash, Khaya African mahogany, Philippine mahogany, sapele African ribbon stripe, spanish cedar, western red cedar, white oak, Douglas fir, and premium vertical-grain Sitka spruce spar stock. *http://www.boulterplywood.com/*

M(aurice). L. Condon Company, Inc., 250 Ferris Avenue, White Plains, NY 10603. Mast- and spar-grade Sitka spruce, Philippine and African mahogany, white cedar, oak, teak, cypress, Douglas fir, and lignum vitae. *http://www.condonlumber.net/*

Edensaw Woods Ltd., 211 Seton Road, Port Townsend, WA 98368. Stocks a large range of plywood for the marine industry, including a Lloyd's of London-rated European-style multi-layered Okoume marine plywood. *http://www.edensaw.com/*

General Hardwoods and Marine Millwork, Inc., 2619 Southwest 2nd Avenue, Ft. Lauderdale, FL 33315. *http://www.genhardwoods.com/*

Harbor Sales Company, 100 Harbor Court, Sudlersville, MD 21668. Teak, cedar, Douglas fir, mahogany, and marine-grade plywood. *http://www.harborsales.net/*

Logan Lumber Company, 1635 Tappan Boulevard, Tampa, FL 33619. *http://www.loganlumber.com/*

Maine Coast Lumber, 17 White Birch Lane, York, ME 03909. Marine plywoods including sapele African mahogany, African okoume, marine meranti; type 1 glue layups including exterior okoume, ribbon stripe sapele, teak, marine fir, Honduras mahogany, and Luan. *http://www.mainecoastlumber.com/*

McEwen Lumber Company, a division of Hood Industries, 3160 West 45th Street, Jacksonville, FL 32209 and twelve other locations. Teak, Honduras mahogany, and many other species. *http://www.hoodindustries.com/*

Medley Hardwoods, 7182 Northwest 77th Terrace, Miami, FL 33136. *http://medleyhardwoodsinc.com/*

Merritt Marine Supply, 2621 NE 4th Avenue, Pompano Beach, FL 33064. Marine plywood. *http://www.merrittsupply.com/*

A. E. Sampson & Son, 171 Camden Road, Warren, ME 04864. Douglas fir, hickory, oak, poplar, walnut, pine, Jabota (Brazilian cherry), and European steamed beech. Maine species: ash, eastern white pine, Norway pine, hard maple, soft maple, yellow birch, red birch, and cherry. *http://www.aesampsonandson.com/*

Shell Lumber Company, 2733 SW 27th Avenue, Miami, FL 33133. *http://www.shelllumber.com/Shell_Lumber.html/*

West Wind Hardwoods, Inc., #5-10189 McDonald Park Road, Sidney, BC Canada V8L-5X5; 1-800-667-2275. Domestic, European, and Asian marine plywoods. *http://www.westwindhardwood.com/*

Wooden Boat Shop, 6569 Gracely Drive, P.O. Box 33013, Cincinnati, OH 45233. Marine plywood. http://www.woodenboatshop.com/

Yukon Lumber Company, 520 West 22nd Street, Norfolk, VA 23517. *http://www.yukonlumber.com/*

Fiberglass and Other Hull Materials

3A Composites, 108 Fairway Court, Northvale, NJ 07647. Manufacturer of Baltek plywood and Airex core materials. *http://www.3acomposites.com/*

Defender Industries, Inc., 42 Great Neck Road, Waterford, CT 06385. Complete online catalog, including synthetic fabrics and resins. *http://www.defender.com/*

Fiberglass Coatings, Inc., 4301A 34th Street N, St. Petersburg, FL 33714. Extensive line of synthetic fabrics and resins. *http://www.fgci.com/*

Fiberglass Supply, 11824 Water Tank Road, Burlington, WA 98233. *http://www.fiberglasssupply.com/*

Merritt Marine Supply, 2621 NE 4th Avenue, Pompano Beach, FL 33064. Fiberglass products and marine plywood. *http://www.merrittsupply.com/*

Seemann Composites, Inc., 12481 Glascock Drive, Gulfport, MS 39503. Manufacturer of C-Flex fiberglass. *http://seemanncomposites.com/cflex.html/*

Metal Fasteners

Anchor Staple & Nail Company, 28 Blanchard Place, Wakefield, RI 02879. *http://www.anchorsssn.com/*

Chesapeake Marine Fasteners, P.O. Box 6691, 110 Compromise Street, Annapolis, MD 21401. *http://www.chesfast.com/*

Duck Trap Woodworking (Walter J. Simmons), P.O. Box 88, Lincolnville Beach, ME 04849. *http://www.duck-trap.com/*

W. L. Fuller, Inc., 7 Cypress Street, Warwick, RI 02888. *http://www.wlfuller.com/*

Hamilton Marine, 155 East Main Street, Searsport, ME 04974. *http://www.hamiltonmarine.com/*

Jamestown Distributors, 17 Peckham Drive, Bristol, RI 02809. All types of marine fasteners. *http://www.jamestowndistributors.com/*

Pacific Fasteners U.S., Inc., 18866 72nd Avenue South, Kent, WA 98032. Online catalog. *http://www.pacificfasteners.com/*

Adhesives

Aircraft Spruce and Specialty Company, 225 Airport Circle, Corona, CA 92882 and 452 Dividend Drive, Peachtree City, GA 30269. Glues. *http://www.aircraftspruce.com/*

Fiberglass Coatings, Inc., 4301A 34th Street N, St. Petersburg, FL 33714. Epoxy adhesives. *http://www.fgci.com/*

Glen-L.com, 9152 Rosecrans, Bellflower, CA 90706. Poxy-Grip epoxy. *http://www.glen-l.com/*

Gougeon Brothers, Inc., P.O. Box 908, Bay City, MI 48707. Formulates and manufactures *WEST SYSTEM* and *PRO-SET* marine-grade epoxies used around the world in boatbuilding and boat repair. *http://www.westsystem.com/ss/* or *http://www.prosetepoxy.com/*

Industrial Plastics & Paints, 150-12571 Bridgeport Road, Richmond, BC, Canada V6V 2N5. G2 and Cold Cure epoxies. *http://www.ippnet.com/*

Jamestown Distributors, 17 Peckham Drive, Bristol, RI 02809. *http://www.jamestowndistributors.com/*

System Three Resins, 3500 West Valley Highway North, Suite 105, Auburn, WA 98001-2436. System Three epoxy tolerates low temperatures and high humidity; stocked by a number of marine supply stores, or available direct. *http://www.systemthree.com/*

Wicks Aircraft Supply, 410 Pine Street, Highland, IL 62249. Epoxies. *http://www.wicksaircraft.com/*

Oars and Oarlocks

Barkley Sound Marine, 3073 Vanhorne Road, Qualicum Beach, BC, Canada V9K 1X3. *http://barkleysoundoar.com/*

Caviness Woodworking, Inc., 200 North Aycock Avenue, Calhoun City, MS. *http://www.cavinesspaddles.com/*

Duck Trap Woodworking (Walter J. Simmons), P.O. Box 88, Lincolnville Beach, ME 04849. Plans for making oars. *http://www.duck-trap.com/*

NRS, 2009 S Main Street, Moscow, ID 83843. *http://www.nrsweb.com/*

Sea-Dog Line Corporation, P.O. Box 479, Everett, WA 98206. *http://www.sea-dog.com/*

Shaw & Tenney, 20 Water Street, Orono, ME 04473. *http://www.shawandtenney.com/*

Paintbrushes

Elder & Jenks, Inc., 148 East 5th Street, Bayonne, NJ 07002. *http://www.elderandjenks.com/*

Epifanes North America Inc., 70 Water Street, Thomaston, ME 04861. *http://www.epifanes.com/*

Hamilton Marine, 155 East Main Street, Searsport, ME 04974. Badger and badger-type brushes. *http://www.hamiltonmarine.com/*

West Marine (home office), 500 Westridge Drive, Watsonville, CA 95076. *http://www.westmarine.com/*

WoodenBoat Store, P.O. Box 78, Naskeag Road, Brooklin, ME 04616. *http://www.woodenboatstore.com/*

Wooster Brush Company, P.O. Box 6010, 604 Madison Avenue, Wooster, OH 44691. *http://www.woosterbrush.com/*

Paint and Other Coatings

Epifanes North America Inc., 70 Water Street, Thomaston, ME 04861. *http://www.epifanes.com/*

International Paint Company, 6001 Antoine Drive, Houston, TX 77091. *http://www.international-marine.com/*

Pettit Paint Company, 36 Pine Street, Rockaway, NJ 07366. *http://www.pettitpaint.com*

Progress Paint, 300 Envoy Circle, Suite 302, Louisville, KY 40299. *http://www.progresspaint.com/*

Rodda Paint Company, 6107 N Marine Drive, Portland, OR 97203. *http://www.roddapaint.com/*

Building Our Own Dinghy in a Weekend Workshop (Excerpts)

—Mary Kay Benjamin and Anthony Flores*

We had always flirted with the idea of building our own dinghy. One day we noticed a sign at the local YWCA: "Build Your Own Dinghy in One Weekend." A course description mentioned some details: "Bring a friend, pliers, and a pair of scissors. Begin Friday evening, and row out Sunday afternoon."

After examining a sample dinghy exhibited in the Y's lobby, we decided this was it, and registered for the next session. On the appointed day, we were instructed to go to the woodworking shop, where we met our instructor, Redjeb "Reggie" Jordania, designer of the UQBAR family of superlight 7-, 8-, and 10-foot prams to row or sail. We were to build the 8-foot rowing model. There were

BEST BETS

The best of all possible things to buy, see, and do in this best of all possible cities.

By Nancy McKeon and Corky Pollan

Three Days Before the Mast

Bring scissors, pliers, a paintbrush, and a putty knife to the Y.W.C.A. on Friday at six and go home with an eight-foot rowing dinghy on Sunday at five. Redjeb Jordania (below), who conducts this brand-new workshop and who teaches boatbuilding at South Street Seaport, assures us that the ability to hammer a nail is all the skill necessary. His "Uqbar" dinghies are put together by the stitch-and-glue method. Pre-cut parts are assembled with copper wire and then glued together with epoxy-resin glue. There will be three weekend classes—March 19, 20, 21; April 23, 24, 25; and May 14, 15, 16—and each course costs $400, materials included. Register now. *Y.W.C.A. /610 Lexington Avenue, at 53rd Street/755-4500, ext. 60*

NEW YORK/MARCH 8, 1982

also two other couples who were going to build their own boat alongside us. . . .

The amazing thing is that in a very short time—2 hours—the boat was assembled, ready to be glued! First, we chamfered the hull panels' edges, to help align them properly. In 15 minutes we were done, and the hull assembly began. This was done by threading 6" lengths of copper wire through matching, pre-drilled holes, twisting them on the outside, and then tightening the whole thing. It was very convenient to work in pairs, since as each side plank was attached to the hull, one of us could push the wire through while the other would hold the still-wobbly assembly to counteract the bending moment.

It was a bit difficult to tighten the wire at the forefoot, and we could not finish bridging small gaps. But to work under the direction of a professional is reassuring: Reggie explained that small gaps there, of less than ¼", were of no consequence, as long as they were even on both sides. These would be filled in with epoxy putty when filleting, for a 100%-strength bond. . . . Since we had time left that first evening, we glued on the seat risers and the keelson.

Epoxies, Fillets, and Old Clothes

Saturday morning we proceeded to spread an epoxy fillet over the copper wire, on the inside. We learned to mix small quantities of resin, hardener, and thickeners to a putty-like consistency, and to apply it as smoothly as possible. This is not easy, particularly because we had to work relatively fast: institutions such as the Y are always overheated, and the woodshop proved no exception, despite two fans. We saw firsthand how rapidly epoxy hardening time diminishes at increased temperatures.

But Reggie, again, reassured us. He explained that the resin hardens faster in the pot than it does once spread, and that one can always add epoxy to already hardened resin with no loss of strength. But he also noted that if you do let it harden, you'll then have to sand it smooth, instead of just shaping it in its gooey state.

The next step was to install the seats, a straightforward process, since supports and seats were pre-cut. We had to shave a little from the forward and aft seats to make them fit, dry-installed them first, then removed all parts, coated matching surfaces with epoxy, and glued them in place. We went home Saturday evening quite tired—backs really stiff from bending all day over the boat—but very happy. Our own dinghy was indeed well on its way to becoming the real thing, and not a dream any longer!

Finishing and Fairing

The last day of our weekend project started with snipping off the copper wire-ties, pulling out whatever pieces would come free, and then fairing the seams and rounding them on the outside. Holes and gouges were filled with epoxy, fiberglass tape was affixed over all outside seams with clear epoxy resin, and the transom doublers were installed. A groove was chiseled out for the skeg; two bolts drilled through from the inside, in conjunction with the epoxy, held it in place permanently. The group adjourned for lunch, amazed at how people so different and with varying levels of skill could nevertheless work at very similar speeds!

The last steps in the afternoon were to glue on the bottom runners (to protect the boat against wear and tear while dragging it up and down a beach) and rubrails. The boat was finished! Of course, it was still in a rough stage, but it was ready for the cosmetic work, which we did later, at home. Most people leave the boat bright, but we elected to paint it. Oarlocks and towing eye were also added at that stage. These dinghies can be modified for sailing at any time, and we plan to do so soon.

We spent a long and hardy season with this excellent rowing pram. She has shown herself very sturdy indeed, as well as practical, and, unless some pirate grabs her, we expect she'll tag along for many years to come.

Reprinted from The Amateur Boat Builder

An Uqbar 8 with a clip-on leeboard in lieu of a daggerboard.

PROFILE AND HALF-BREADTH

scale: ⅛" = 1"

Appendix D
I Built My Own Dinghy
—John A. Russell, Jr.*

A friend had constructed an Uqbar pram using plans published by the Back 'n Forth Company of New York City. The end product was a nine-foot, flat bottom, lightweight plywood boat with a 4½-foot beam with high sides and three seats. Two interesting features of his boat were its unusual construction method and that it had space under the seats for positive flotation. I tested my friend's boat and decided it met our requirements, so I borrowed his plans, purchased the materials, and started to work.

The Back 'n Forth plans are based on a construction technique of pulling six precut plywood panels together by twisting many short lengths of wire and gradually pulling the panels into place. The panels are permanently fastened together with reinforced epoxy fillets. Epoxy fillets are then installed, permanently fastening the plywood pieces together to form a strong box. Exposed portions of the wire ties are removed before seams are taped and aren't visible in the finished boat. This construction technique is known as the "stitch-and-glue" method.

Cross bracing, provided by the seats and their support, and stiffness, provided by the filleted plywood junctions, result in a lightweight boat with no internal framing. The filleted seams and fiberglass tape on the outside virtually assure freedom from leaks. I clamped together and glued most of the other parts (with the exception of the external rubrails), avoiding permanent screws or fasteners.

I modified the original design by eliminating the partial inwales in favor of mounting pads for each oarlock socket. (The partial inwales called for in the original design would have provided sufficient gunwale stiffness as well as a sturdy oarlock socket mount.) I also installed braces in each corner of the boat at the gunwales, more for appearance and handholds than for strength. Because I consider a dinghy safety equipment, I installed closed-cell Styrofoam providing approximately 150 pounds of positive flotation. It's located under the fore and aft seats and is totally enclosed in plywood.

The dinghy plans called for treating all wooden surfaces with epoxy, producing a waterproof and very attractive finish on the birch plywood. Unfortunately, ultraviolet rays from the sun damage epoxy, so all exposed surfaces are painted or varnished. I used polyurethane marine topside enamel, Hatteras white, to match the creamy color of our San Juan sailboat.

Throughout the project, I chose WEST SYSTEM epoxy products manufactured by Gougeon Brothers of Bay City, Michigan. I followed their instructions for adding fillers and thickeners to the basic resin in making glue, filler, or filleting stock. I needed less than two quarts.

Constructing the dinghy took approximately 100 hours over a three-month period. This enjoyable project has satisfied my urge to construct a dinghy, and the finished boat has produced a feeling of personal achievement. Its trim lines have received compliments from both boating and cabinetmaking friends. It will add to our future cruising pleasure, and it may even provide a source of entertainment for visiting grandchildren.

*This article reprinted from The Ensign

Index